Not A *MISMATCH*

Not A
MISMATCH

by

Dr. Sammy O. Joseph

Pulse Publishing House

Contents

Acknowledgement

On behalf of *PULSE Publishing House*, I do gratefully acknowledge the overwhelming majority of friends – too many to name here who aided my judgment in choosing this book's back cover design. I somehow trust that the world of my readership audience will agree with your choice, as the very best one!

Bryn Davies, a very dear family friend whose dedication and preference for perfection shows forth glaringly in his graphic illustrations of the majority of my books; thanks for dedicatedly carving out time for me at the time the preparation for your wedding in March was so close. On behalf of the Josephs, I seize the opportunity therefore to pray you and your bride, Lucy, a "Happily Hereafter."

The major part of this work originated from a significant proportion of friends, readership and listening audiences of all backgrounds and cultures who had wanted me to produce a comprehensive work that focuses on the issues facing modern relationships: marriages, family-siblings, peers and so on, as it pertains to the peculiarities of western cultural orientation. I thank the *PULSE Publishing*

House for her part availing to me large portions of my earlier work: *Destroying the Power of Delay: Possessing Your Canaan*, to be excerpted, quoted or re-produced in some parts of this work! I also acknowledge those friends who gave me the permission to publish their real-life stories even though names, identities and locations have been changed to protect privacy.

Finally as is my custom, I acknowledge the two very wonderful young ladies and three handsome gentlemen I am so privileged to – with every ounce of godly pride – call my children: Gabby, Dave, Danny, Prissy 'Co-co' and our dear Apostle, Paul; THANK YOU all so very much, for your exceptional encouragement to me to perform the ministry of the Lord, to which I was called! May your oil overflow, always. Amen.

Chapter 1

Introduction

"You are invaluable no matter what you've been through; you're not a misfit — or a mismatch!"

— SAMMY O. JOSEPH

Mid-summer of 2014, I had visited the 'open evening' of the school of advanced learning of my older daughter's choice in the company of my family. There, I had been presented with ample opportunities as parents usually are, to inquire about life at — and the ethos of — the institution. If you had read any of my other books, you would have noticed my gifts of learning and imparting knowledge in my field of expertise.

I'd struck a somewhat interesting conversation with one

of the would-be lecturers. His name is Peter Covington. A divorcee author as at the time of my writing, he lectures Sociology at the institution. When I had asked him of his opinion on what repercussions divorce has, particularly on children of divorced parents in our generation, he'd gently unscrewed the tap of his wealth of experience and learning which I am sure I could compose into a whole, separate title. However, that's not my aim in this work; just one of his statements had stuck with me up until this very moment – and that had mattered to me then, as it does now. (In the same vein, if just one sentence or line of this work sticks with you for the rest of your entire being, I would have succeeded in my aim!) Mr. Covington had said: *"Divorce rates have fallen quite drastically in England and Wales since the past four years – thank goodness in part, to the praise of the Coalition government's austerity measures!"*

Those remarks were meant to be sarcastic, but nevertheless, factual. In England and Wales, largely since their ascending power in 2010, our coalition government has embarked on a series of cost-cutting measures that have re-shaped the society. Whether for the better – or for the worse, I may not be able to tell since I am neither a politician nor an economist! One of those areas affected by the drastic cuts is public funding that used to be freely available to anyone contemplating a divorce. Public Funding had been governed and administered by *Legal Aid*, a department of public funding!

What the expert had said in effect was that the statistical

fact about divorce rates having fallen drastically in England and Wales should *not* be misconstrued to mean that there's more happiness between many a married couple in today's society of multi-ethnicity and cultures. Rather, the harsh economic conditions and the aftermath of choosing the option of divorcing compared with working to better their deteriorating marriages leaves both the *petitioner* and the *respondent* very much worse off economically in most cases, than if they had opted to stay together married – willy-nilly!

Undoubtedly this seems to be a huge score for the law-makers!

While the government's statistics and the *Press* hail her stemming of the endemic problem of divorce as an unprecedented huge plus-factor, the establishment leaves a much mesmerized myriad of counselors, the clergy, classroom teachers and the police a very humongous job of reconciling the many lapses staying-together-married causes!

Am I against lasting marriages?

No!

In fact, one of my objectives in this book it is to encourage married peoples' vows last as long as death do them part. But as long as marriages do *not* last, there will ever continue to be a huge preponderance of varying adverse effects and turmoil left in their wake! These too ought to be remarkably curtailed!

One Major Area State Establishments Have Failed

No lawmaker would ever dare admit that there are many unhappy, unsatisfied, cheating married couples forcibly co-habiting as just mere co-tenants or lodgers. This trend has been up-crawling since the mid 2010's, more than at any other preceding time in our history. This is a societal catastrophe!

You see, read or hear of situations where a divorced couple actually never moved out of *their* former home, yet could somehow strike an economically harmonious tune whilst they merely shared spaces. Occupants I guess had it figured out it would be far cheaper to maintain same home, divorced; rather than pursuing an outright exit. This is also an aberration! Our world has tumbled upside down the moral upright code! We all know the potential outcome of when anyone is dictated unto. Such a resulting outcome is usually the creation of well-formed, rotund, rebel-monsters. These monsters, like foxes, do wreck much havoc.

There exist many unreported cases of twisted, warped, sickening, so-called, cohabiting, hate-relationships where the abuse meted out to *inmates* of such love-hate jail-houses have become so horrendous, inhumane and of preposterous magnitude. In some extreme cases when the law-enforcers had been dispatched in answer to the desperate call of a victim, Police had arrived to gory scenes: brutally murdered spouse, cases of double tragedies, a traumatized child securely locked up in a room

– and a surviving brow-beaten dog secured in the kennel, downstairs!

When tragic situations like these involving surviving child(ren) occur, no matter their ages, long-lasting psychological emotional traumas and damage will happen. Given a short while, the foster, adoption or home systems will turn out tens of thousands of young adults in their early twenties who though, probably managed to get qualified educationally, may have by and large become dysfunctional in their minds and emotions!

It usually takes the grace of God at any given latter date to unknot the many intricate, interwoven years of turmoil and knots – the 'system' could neither unravel nor unknot – that have eventually produced such *complex* young adults! This is the bottom-line inference of mine stemming from my experiences as a counseling minister of God over the past quarter of a century, studying and working with families with upheavals!

When marital homes are in trouble, no matter the disguise and the splash of the 'happiness-paint' we daub on our faces or the expensive perfumes we wear, destinies of individuals are at stake, surrendered to the 'system' – a 'system' which is just a cache of digits, overburdened by societal dysfunctions.

When individuals' psychological codes are tampered with; ultimately, society's and future generations' well-being are endangered! Prevention, therefore from making the wrong decisions in my humble gathering, has always been better than the prescribed cure, divorce for instance, may be expected to produce!

But does divorce — and re-marriage bring a cure and lasting healing?

I very much doubt it.

I do know however of lingering effects a wrong marriage could have on a spouse, ex-spouse, a new spouse, the children — and the society at large!

Every person of marriageable age has a rightful expectation to be married. Sad to say however, *not* everyone of marriageable age may be able to bear up under the demands that meet such high expectations enjoyed in happy marriages. This has been one of my call-out, catch-phrases for the past decade!

I had also like the sociologist-author-lecturer earlier mentioned undergone a bitter divorce with five little children to raise without any form of support from anyone else, but God's alone. I know the huge costs the death of a marriage or spouse accosts. I had experienced first-hand, the importance of life-altering, life-saving, quick decisions amid overpowering torrents of life's currents. By the power of God, I have safely navigated those treacherous meanders. In the past decade alone — 2005 to 2015 — I had made sacrifices that had ensured the turning out to the highest cadre, highly civilized, five young adults whom God Himself have called to co-minister with me in the Gospel ministry. Each of these has over time witnessed great, overpowering, personal conviction and passion from their respective spiritual perspectives. I am writing you therefore, not from an outsider's, 'holier-than-thou' perspective; but from that of an insider's, with a wealth of relevant information that would spin your life right way around, if you would *walk* with me!

Great friendships, relationships and marriages are great; but they do *not* come cheaply! Or do they? Because a potential one in every two of us have not been taught from youthful ages how to prepare to pay the price tags attached to ensuring successful relationships, many adults have made a ship-wreck of their lives – and possibly, others' at such un-imaginably cheap tickets. Unfortunately, these are they who appear before the dressing mirrors of their personal worth as as either mar-ginalized – or mismatched.

My message to you therefore is simple: your adverse life experiences or circumstances do *not* make you irrelevant. In my view, no one should label themselves as "irrel-evant" or "mismatched", let alone adopt that defeatist mental attitude of viewing themselves as already defeated. No matter your background, color, ethnicity or creed, the Creator has your very name written in the palms of His hands – and calls you by that name. You are *not* a misfit. You are *not* mismatched; strength yet avails for your emancipation.

It is with that heart to both prevent and unbind any possible heavy laden you carry that this book has been written. It will be found useful in counseling and rehabilitative therapy of emotional healing, until a full restoration is achieved! I hugely anticipate it turns out exactly as tailored to meet your highest expectations – and indeed, surpass those expectations beyond imaginable success!

Have a happy reading.

Sammy O. Joseph
Birmingham,
ENGLAND.

Chapter 2

Cohabitants of a Fallen World

Dare to make this world a better place than you met it by acts of kindness, a day; everyday!

— SAMMY O. JOSEPH

No one in their rightful working human mind — notice my description of that mind — expects to live in a utopian world; that is, a physical world devoid of pain, hurts, disappointments, anxieties, beleaguered perspirations — and possibly botched expectations. There's *no* such thing as a perfect *earthly* world!

I wrote this page after I had returned from the interment of a close friend and pastor-colleague, Phillip — not his real name — who had departed our world for his eternal residence at an unripe age of 49! Not a single one of us had least expected such a heart-breaking occurrence. Phillip had been a very fit and healthy man all his years until that fateful morning. He had bidden his wife *"Bye, Sweetie"* as she'd departed for work earlier; he had intended to go the church office at about 10 *a.m.* But it never had been.

Phillip was a hard-working, responsible husband, father and community leader. He never left anyone who did encounter him without a joyful impact. He brightened and made the day for many. He was a giver and a philanthropist. He was larger than life – but suddenly, on that fateful morning, he had slumped. One of his sons had dialed *999*. He was soon in the ambulance on his way to the hospital. The doctors on emergency at the *A & E* had split seconds to arrive at a conclusion in an effort to save his life. They had decided he would need a quick neurosurgical operation from which he never came round! His families and us his circle of friends had been plunged into deep heart-wrenching sorrow and grief! His passing had been like a dream from which we still haven't totally recovered!

Bereavement, afflictions, protracted illnesses, separation from a partner / spouse or divorce from marriage, job-loss – and the like could actually threaten to jeopardize and disrupt our smooth livelihood this side of eternity. The accompanying sorrow and the mourning, the sadness and possibly the depression – including self-doubts – that may set in at the onslaught of these mischievous life occurrences sometimes could become ir-reversible, if care is *not* taken!

You Are Not the Label You Wear

Do you know why anyone could be prone to experience the lingering depth and effects of sorrow, sadness, depression and death?

The answer is easy. It is because *they* are inhabitants of the earth. Folk who have trusted the Lord Jesus Christ as Savior and Lord are no longer ordinary inhabitants of this planet. Rather, they are citizens of a greater kingdom – the Kingdom of Heaven.

I'm an optimist – but I'm also a realist. Above all, I'm a believer in Jesus Christ! More, I believe in the continued existence of our world, the need for careful maintenance and replenishment of life, nature and wildlife on the planet. The optimism, realism and depth of my beliefs in the Judeo-Christian God notwithstanding, I'm also of the firm assurance that serenity and utopia will *not* be fully experienced on this present planet earth until the Lord Jesus Christ ascends His throne in His *millennial reign* as prophesied by the prophets of old!

In the interim however, what we all could aim to achieve is intermarrying the contextual existence of continued opportunities that juxtapose the uncertainties associated with being residents of our decadent, yet modern world! Thus, we cannot continue to deny the facts and figures associated with our temporal abode. Some of you already have begun shaking your heads in disagreement: you then make me smile! These are *you* who refuse to recognize just one unfortunate truth – that we are made up of matter and bones which are subject to rottenness and decay, much as *Mother Earth* itself!

Because our outer casements or jackets – that is, our physical bodies – are essentially earthly, terrestrial and mundane; we are bound to *feel*, *touch*, *see*, *sense* and *taste*. We achieve these activities by gainfully employing the use of the five physical senses we discovered we were endowed with at birth – if we are fortunate enough to still possess them, in perfect working order! Ironically though, those physiological body parts may not be working up to *par*! Some senses may be impaired; others, restricted. Because yours may be incapacitated, limited, restrained or restricted to what you could or could not do, citizens of our world are quick to peel off a sticker from a label of many lists dangling in their minds *and* affix on your forehead. Some are unkind enough to even rub it in firmly as to ensure it stays, glued to a conspicuous spotting headline. Even our different governments in different nations use labels. The prison systems of the world, for example, universally employ the use of numbers. Offender-humans are derogatorily reduced to mere numerals to which they must answer. Examiners on the other hand assign numbers to prospective candidates whom they are assessing; each candidate dares not forget his / her examination number. In a similar vein, you wouldn't dare assign just one wrong digit to a bank account!

Do you see what I see? Do you perceive my thoughts?

Affixing Labels, numbers and digits on objects may *not* be inherently wrong, generally speaking; but when they have been employed for derogatory purposes, I may have to become the very first to confidently shoot my right hand up into the air well above my head and demand logical explanations as to *why* that should be! Such terms as "disabled", "dysfunctional", "child with learning difficulty" become common terms of references to adults, young adults or indeed younger children who have somehow, somewhere, fallen short of the *status quo* definition of functionality of the everyday society. But you're *not* a piece of stick-up label. Certainly, God didn't create you as a mere ordinary derogatory set of digits! There's a fire burning in my belly; an anguish in my soul, to get you well past that toll gate of spiritual myopia or astigmatism where you merely only *see* yourself and not the glorious future God has planned for you. Your vision has been blurred, blocked and distorted by the label you've been assigned to wear – which label you have settled for.

Let me bring this a little closer home. Because you have *had* a divorce, for instance, should not allude you to bowing down to be affixed with the *status quo* derogatory label pinned onto other divorcees. God didn't create you a divorcee; that mistake *had* occurred, it had occurred – and belongs in the very past! (I sincerely do hope you realize that some divorces occur, not as a product of a mistake. Some unforeseen mishap could – and do happen). *It had happened* – and now it belongs in the past. Hindsight isn't any good anymore than it serves as a mirror. Excellent drivers mandatorily throw occasional glances at their driving mirrors to help them correctly perceive of their current positions in comparison to other road users. They do not gaze into back-mirrors. They drive, looking at what lies ahead, through a bigger glass called the windshield. Throw an occasional glance backward, if you may – at the experience that felled you – and avert further fall! Ultimately, you drive forward learning from such experiences; moving further and further away from them! You travel forward gainfully using your learning as a handy, reference tool for the future.

Apart from knowing how to deal with the past as a divorcee, in a similar token, you ought to know that your being raised in a single-parent family already carries an unspoken societal expectation that *you* must fall short in *certain* areas of life's endavors!

But I beg to strictly differ!

Only *you* in your psychological differential may reduce *you* to the label of 'second-class' citizenry. *You* could – if you like – actually downgrade to a mere 'third-class' member of the society still, just merely by your inference upon the color of your skin. *You* would have become mismatched in *your* very own little mind! Why should that be when the One who created, formed and knew you from your mother's womb says: *"I create no misfits; nor mismatches. I declare the end from the very beginning."*[1] Jehovah is His name. His labels alone have I by faith conditioned my mind to believe, receive, accept and wear. I do not only wear them; I make a public display of them. He it is Who makes me who I am in Him! Not any man's report, label or numerology!

Because of the afore-said, therefore, it would behoove me to cast the die on the word *'mismatch'* as I intend it to be used in this book, before your mind renders it his / her own way. I have *not* used that word *'mismatch'* loosely – but as you leaf through these pages, it is in my greatest dis-interest to 'label' a particular scenario as it pertains *your* situation, relationships, friendships and / or marriage – if you are married! In other words, I wouldn't be happy to have you overcome by guilt, if you perceive your social standing as lesser than the societal *status quo!* In fact, that is the essential reason I have titled the book: *Not A Mismatch!* Yes, you just read it: *'Not A Mismatch.'*

You're *not* a mismatch – neither are you a misfit. You're *not* dull. You're *not* what name the bullies and haters call you – whoever they are! Bullies' and haters' name-tags and words are simply symptomatic of what underlying issues personally unceasingly nag at them. You are who the Heavenly Father God says you are! Simple. Ditto. No arguments. That alone suffices!

Listen, there is *no* such life or relationship that is perfect. If you're looking for one, you will surely find it on the yonder side of eternity! Take for example if you were to fall in love with an angel from heaven, you would be the one that would tarnish his holiness! In other words, there is yet to be a human that is so "angelic" as to be bereft of their humaneness. Only Jesus Christ excelled and broke that barrier-limit on mankind! He had been – and will ever be – the only *One* human Who had lived (and will ever live) far above the corruptibility of sin of this present life! No one else dares attain His untainted, unblemished record of their own accord!

Sometimes, without any warning – or a foreseeable reason, a life-changing event occurs. A new-baby develops some nameless, life-threatening illness. He or she may die. A friendship suddenly begins drawing farther apart – and the concerned people may never reconcile. A spouse suddenly awakens one day and flees the home without any tangible reason: in their humaneness, they have hurriedly scribbled on a piece of paper a note that says they are *not* returning home and would prefer to *not* be traced! That kind of a pathetic scenario places the abiding spouse in a limbo, doesn't it? Here's another equally emotive scene: a well-loved hitherto secured company suddenly goes into administration. It receives no bail-out money from the government or the state. It just went burst! Masses were laid off, compulsorily made redundant. To make matters worse, the company won't even pay any employee a penny of their entitled redundancy-package; it simply hasn't got the funds!

If you were to experience any of the described situations above, would you reckon it a fair deal to label yourself a 'misfit' because of what you suffered? Should you heap blames of unworthiness on yourself if you were the one being walked out on in a marriage? Doubtless, you are pained – but I am asking *if* you could refrain from heaving heavier emotional, psychological or physical burden upon yourself because of your experience of an ill-dished circumstance of life!

My employment of the word *mismatch* in this book therefore could be synonymous to such other words as: *unequal, uneven, unevenly-shared, disproportionate, lop-sided* or *unfair!*

Mismatched at a very Tender Age

There are many reasons why our experiences in this less-than-perfect world may have resulted into situations that seem like *mismatches. Unequal. Uneven. Unevenly-shaped. Disproportionate. Lopsided* – or even *unfair.* This book – while not attempting to exhaustively examine all these possibilities – will nevertheless turn on *halogen lights* on a few *"spots in your feasts of charity"*, as author Apostle Jude had aptly, fittingly described in his letter *(Jude 12).*

Certainly, I am aware that the Word of God, the Bible, teaches the one huge root-cause why our world is so full of apparitions looking like *mismatches* is as a result of sin. Sin arose as a result of man's treachery in the Garden of Eden. It affects over 7 billion human cohabitants on planet earth, today! You probably would have – at least once before – heard of that Utopian Garden of Eden. (In case you had not until now, I would request you to read the full account in the first few chapters of Moses' first book: *Genesis).*

The second major reason your circumstances may turn unfavorably *mismatched* is credited to poor decisions. *Your* poor decisions – or some insane person's poor decision consequences of which had come to bear down heavily upon you. Poor decisions are most often based upon the mirages of misalignment and misinformation. Because you are either *misinformed* or *misaligned* in bad friendships and relationships; or have come to *accept* mirages as reality when in fact, they are not, *you* are sometimes prone to make irredeemably, remarkably poor choices!

Now, if these were true – and they are; the fallen, rebellious nature in men and women gravitate them ever lower and closer to the rottenness called *sin*. We by nature are beings that would preferentially choose rottenness over wholesomeness, lies over truth and unrighteousness over righteousness! Now that's mind boggling, isn't it?

While *"the whole world lies in wickedness"* and depravity as God's word says in *1 John 5:19*, God still yet guides His children to circumvent the paralytic troubles inherent in this life – particularly those pernicious troubles wrapped up in wrong choices. This He does through the ministry of the Holy Spirit! Oh, it is possible that a good lass may fall for a bad boy *not* because she essentially wants to; her poor choice may have been set in motion from the abuse she had suffered in childhood. I have seen that happen many a time. Take for example the story of Nina.

Nina (not her real name), a friend of mine in her late-forties is a Cherokee American native from Georgia, United States of America. She has coursing her veins a mixture of the kind and rugged Irish blood via her mother's ancestry and her father's fierce and rugged

Native American. She is the second of three children: two sisters and a brother whom she is older than by seven years. Their mother had died two years after the baby brother had been born. Shortly afterwards, their father had become depressed and had decided to go both offensive and abusive on his daughters. He had engaged in incestuous relationship, first, with the eldest daughter, aged 11 until she'd run away at 15. He had then found himself a girlfriend who had been twenty-one years older than him – and had abandoned and neglected his second daughter Nina 11, and the little fella, aged 4. He'd drank heavily and had visited home only on weekends. Nina had assumed the roles of a mother and big sister to her four-year old little brother when dad had been absent, seeking love. She had locked him up in the basement of their huge house, had milked the cows – and had gone to sell the milk, delivering on foot to homes on an average early morning total journey of six miles, thrice weekly before she had gone to school. They had lived on a large acreage of farm settlement with no house in range, miles on end! Her little life had been a misery.

From her weekly wages, she had fended for both herself and her little brother! Her life was a closely-guarded, closed-circuit secret. Whenever father had sauntered home on weekends, those had been weekends a step away from *very* hell! He had incestuously violated Nina, tortured and threatened her with severe whip-lashes if she ever told anyone his misdeeds. *"It's both our secret"* she used to her him say, in her very own words to me!

After about three years of an unceasing abuse, Nina at 14 had mustered enough strength to confide in her best class-mistress. The *CPS* had been called – and both she and little fella had been fostered in faraway Florida.

Father had vanished into thin air!

Life had seemed to be so good in Nina's mid-teens; but there had remained unresolved bitterness and rebellion on the inside of her. As she'd grown older under new foster parents, she had partied hard, smoked weed and gotten high on banned substances. Bad boys with attitudes made her nights cozy and complete. She had become an epitome of *wildness* by 17. On one of her most memorable dates, she had been smitten by her high school heart-throb. They had gotten married a few months after they had discovered they were expecting a child.

The next three years saw an addition to the family of the birth of another baby girl. Nina's husband had unilaterally decided to enlist in the US Marine Corps. He had been deployed out of reach. While on deployment, he had gained taste for wild bar women; he had never returned home to Nina and their two little daughters. Nina had been heartbroken – and had had to seek divorce from her husband at age 21.

Now a single mother, life had been proving far more than a joke. Bottles of drinks had downed her heartache and pains. She had struggled to cope with raising two little girls on her own. But the 'low' vicissitudes of life soon had proved too much to handle: she had started to abandon her daughters with neighbors more frequently, in search of love and sex at the bars and clubs. She had craved to be loved, appropriately!

Soon, she had been introduced to a fine looking young man who had at first seemed nice, caring and kind. No sooner had she vulnerably availed him with sex had he massively taken advantage of her! Despite many pregnancy-prevention techniques, she had fallen pregnant, again – and for the sake of not raising the child alone, had agreed to marry him. But soon, abuse and violations had commenced *"far worse than my father had meted to me"* she had stated to me, tears coursing down her cheeks. It had dawned upon her then that her second marriage had proceeded so fast onto the rocky pathways she had sang and danced to in *Rock 'n Roll* numbers on the dance-floors! At first, she had thought she would weather through, so she had endured much more gross abuse that doesn't fit my description here! After their tenth year of marriage, she had called it quits – and had been granted a second divorce!

In the interim, God had been planning in the background that all her struggles would tally together for good. Her family's pastor had gone through finding a pin in the haystacks, making efforts through the various agencies to find her – and her younger brother – not knowing that Nina's family had increased. He had been praying for their family.

Through the elderly pastor's gentle persuasive powers, Nina's heart had been touched by the Lord: she had opened her heart up to the Lord to save her soul. She had become a brand new creature. An erstwhile pastor who knows the importance of discipleship and training had begun making arrangements to relocate her, her children and brother back from Florida to Georgia. She had soon been enrolled at a Management College – and had graduated! Nina had found employment, bought a home of her own and had been doing well in mentoring her teenaged-daughters and their little brother in a deliberate, mindful attempt to nip in the bud any signs of misinformation, misalignment and illusory effects of mirages on their pathways!

While at work someday, news reached her that her biological father – and the granddad to her kids – whom neither she nor her children had re-met in over two decades laid dying of prostate cancer at the hospice. This lady of courage had resolved within her to nurse him for the rest of his few days. She had moved him home to live with her and her three children. Anytime she had been at work, she'd employed the services of paid carers who had taken turns to care for the weak, old man. Those few days had translated into three years. Three beautiful years within which an offender had received the forgiveness of the offended – and much more, that of the Savior that had saved Nina herself, years earlier! Nina's older sister and her family too had been re-established with their 'old man'.

One morning after caring for her father, he had specially requested Nina to ring her siblings: the older sister and their little brother. He had told them his angel had been dispatched – and had been present in the room to usher him on his next journey. Nina had quickly obliged. Within minutes, all his three children – and seven grandchildren – had clutched his hands and said a prayer with him. He'd then blessed them each before slipping into eternity. *"He had held onto my hand – and had appeared to have dosed off in a peaceful sleep! But he had crossed into eternity,"* Nina had remembered to add!

This beautiful end to her father's historical chapter remains an oasis of strength to Nina up until today! Whenever she reminisces, she believes *"if only children's foundations be set square and straight, there would be lesser needs for mismatches arriving from misinformation, misalignment or the mind's acceptance of mirages as reality in our world!"*

Chapter 3

When Life Requires a Critical Re-appraisal

"Extreme remedies are very appropriate for extreme diseases."

— *Aphorisms;* Hippocrates, 460 BC – 370 BC.

Both the widow of late Phillip and the larger circle of family and friends – not forgetting Nina had had to confront the subject of dealing with grief in their respective lives. Like forgiveness, experiencing, dealing with – and healing from grief *cannot* be hushed; neither can it be demanded from the bereaved! This is because we grieve quite significantly differently, one from the other. We also heal, in the same indicative trends, from our respective unpleasant individual experiences. (And may I just quickly quip here that the act of grieving is *not* an illness to be ashamed of; rather, it is an intrinsic part of life on earth!)

Hippocrates, a Greek physician considered by many to be "the Father of Medicine" in one of his writings, *Precepts* once said: *"Healing is a matter of time."*

Though the Greek scholar may have scored with physical healings as being able to be healed in just a matter of time; you and I do know that emotional hurts and wounds may *not* necessarily be healed in time, except drastic safe-keeping measures are put in place. On that note, I wholeheartedly believe with Hippocrates' statement quoted at the beginning of the chapter that extreme remedies are indeed appropriate for extreme diseases! Because of this fact, I would love to – in this chapter – devote some time to understudying 'How long is long enough for mourners to mourn before they are healed'?

Now, the twenty-fifth chapter of the book *1 Samuel* opens with the unpleasant news of the death of Prophet Samuel followed by the overwhelming national mourning held in his honor by all Israel – including in particular, David his protégé. David probably had felt the impact of his inestimable loss, more than anyone at that time. He would have realized the importance of the treasured physical and spiritual values Prophet Samuel had offered him. Yet, all these had suddenly *'vaporized'*. That kind of a loss can only call for a drastic reaction in any bereaved!

After having witnessed such a poignant funeral service for my belated friend Pastor Philip, these were the very words that I had posted onto my social media space:

"With my final respect to my late dear friend paid a few hours ago, I stood there among many at his final resting place, hot tears caressing my cheeks on a cold, wet autumnal morning! I RENEWED my conscious decision made many years ago – three decades to be exact – to continue to SOW my life away, investing it into the Kingdom!

Someday – probably in death – all mortals will bend to the sway of the law of Sowing and Reaping! Sow your life. Hoard or safely tuck yours away in false hopes and comforts materialism promises! The choice is entirely yours. Wise people however don't wait until death to learn what to do with their lives, talents and gifts!

So HELP ME GOD to finish well!"

When Reality Check Hits

In my counseling with people from different cultures of the world since over a quarter of a century this year 2015; from Europe to Africa, the Americas to Asia, one undeniable denominator is common to all peoples stricken by bereavement or illness. That common denominator is that we all grieve!

We may grieve in slightly different ways, some for shorter or longer periods of time; but undeniably, all humans grieve. Our rights and high expectations to succeed, be celebrated and stay on an adrenalin surge of exclamatory, victorious shouts however needed being tempered too, by such a preparedness to expect someday, to grieve! That's only fair!

"Why should that be?", you ask!

The reason is simple. By the same token that the Rolls Royce car manufacturer for instance had created an exotic, state-of-the-art comfy car and had been mindful to not neglect the importance of building within her designs, strong shock-absorbers; that's the likewise same reason we also should teach from very tender years the necessity of building within our emotional fiber, the grim, abject reality of grief.

I have met and talked with very finely educated minds of both sexes who are professionals in their areas of specializations who are still traumatized by the effects of grief they had either suffered or experienced whilst they were younger; consequences which still mess up their emotions in their mid-forties. Some are still being embarrassed by the unpredictability of their irrational, erratic behaviors stemming from such mishaps that had left them shaken up until today!

Jackie is a blonde Caucasian lady of English descent whose unmarried parents had separated while she had been a mere three-year-old toddler. She was the only female, youngest of five children whose ages were averagely spaced, three years apart! Her parents had parted ways – and gone ahead to meet and marry new spouses; her dad had sired new children with his new wife.

Jackie's step-dad was a compulsive gambler – and a controlling drunk of a man. Jackie's mom, now 75 vividly remembers her husband as a very abusive man who had physically attacked Jackie and her two older sons. In fairness to him, he seemed to have been a troubled man himself, having been sexually abused while he had been fostered as a youth. He had not treated better his older two children from his earlier failed marriage.

As they grew up, Jackie and her two older brothers trembled at the husky voice of their authoritarian step-dad. Jackie's mom's frame – and her voice – were still as tiny as they had been over four decades ago. *"So also were my redemptive powers to rescue my children from the roaring lion-head I had married,"* she quips rather enthusiastically!

Today at 43, Jackie, shrugs at anyone who dares advise her. She just couldn't be bothered to firmly establish a successful working relationship with anyone above her. Neither could she keep a romantic relationship with any man for longer than three months since 21 – even though she has a great personality and a huge propensity to love, from my keen observation. Love just kept eluding her. Since about hitting 30, she had become increasingly lonely and suicidal. Even though she is pretty and highly educated, she confided in me, *"what a pretty messed-up, pretty lady I am upstairs!"*

When asked what she opines in a reflective retrospect, might be responsible for her poor, *less than par* relational skills in her adult life, she had honestly responded: *"My life had caved in when I'd realized my father had left us – and it had later dawned on me that he may never return for me … The little Daddy's girl in me had since missed – and still misses him, very badly!"*

Could it be that Jackie's reality check has hit a *crescendo*?

Very much possibly so!

Jackie had been right! Her father had never been a part of her growing-up life again, until just about a couple of years ago that they had been re-united. *"Daddy had met a grown, stranger lady,"* she said amidst sobs; *"but I'd love him still to see me as his lil' girl!"*

Jackie's 77 year-old father and she continue to work hard to recoup their lost decades. As I write, they should be meeting at one of the *Starbucks* stores in the city, working at re-building the bridges of their relationships. Their meetings continue to be a great therapy tool against the emotional damage fears of abandonment and control had passed onto Jackie's soul by the men who *had been* – and *had not been* but *ought to have been* in her life!

If for Jackie's sake alone, I would never relent in advocating through every possible means, the necessity of fathers' presence in the lives of their children. It is mandatory that fathers continue to play active roles in their children's lives – if it is established that they would not be in any way threats to those children's love and affection!

Honestly speaking, I am least bothered if you and your ex-wife or partner couldn't see eyeball to eyeball; but for the sake of decency, the stable emotional health and healthy social futures of these children, kindly agree on a workable pathway on how you would both be there for your children – socially, emotionally, financially and spiritually!

To those fine women who deliberately manipulate the courts and the 'system' to estrange children from developing positive relationships with their fathers, shame on you! May I just pronounce it into your inner cochleae that your madness today would doubtless estrange your peace farther from you in your old age, if you continue to keep denying these children vital opportunities to bond with their fathers. Truth not only always has had its own ways of catching up with – but overtaking – all lies in just a matter of 18 years. You will remember reading that on this page, I promise you!

Seriously, had I more influence on those law-makers and politicians at the top decision-making body of the education sector, I would mandate the topic of *Grief* be taught from its very rudimentary concepts to the elementary through tertiary levels of education, nationwide! Children – and young adults – must be well prepared and expected to appropriately appreciate the lives, friendships and loves of what and who are there in their little lives. This curriculum, I envisage, would help them cope with the distress mourning *any* loss could cause. My proposition would also create an atmosphere of curtailing the excesses at both ends of the spectrum: blocking out the pain of grieving altogether and the morbidity of over-grieving!

More on the Subject of Grief

Grief was an integral part of the after-effects of that original sin that had blighted our species from our ancestral parents, Adam and Eve. Of course, as said earlier, the likelihood of mismatches arriving from *misinformation, misalignment in choices* and the mind's *acceptance of mirages as reality* would doubtless continue to hunt us all if the roots of sinful corruption are not totally exhumed! Take my word, grieving too needed being correspondingly handled that it does *not* result into negativity!

So may I inquire: "How do *you* handle grief?"

- Do you *suppress* it, adopting an English, stiff-upper-lip attitude, sucking it up?, or;

- Do you become an *inconsolable*, emotional, hot mess like Rachel of Jerusalem in prophet Jeremiah's days *(Jeremiah 31:15)*?, or

- Do you become so *overwhelmed* with so much grief that you transcend into a broken, sick vessel of no earthly good?, or;

- Do you grieve *appropriately*?

Needless to repeat, individuals reserve the right to grieve.

People may grieve according to family traditions, societal traditional customs – or personal requirements. Whichever way you have chosen to grieve, my thoughts are that you should *not* suppress your grief or mourning. Doing so could undo you pathologically, damaging some of your internal organs. So also is over-grieving: I would be glad to ensure that you do *not* become surfeited with the negative emotions associated with over-grieving. Because of the possibilities of verging on these extremities, balance therefore ought to be the appropriate watchword, here. Pure, sheer, common-sense balance – which I am aware, may *not* be common. It certainly had not been accessible even to the caliber of a man such as King David when he had remained inconsolable at the assassination of Absalom, his handsome, fairy-tale son, to the detriment of a whole kingdom being lost to anarchy *(2 Samuel 18:32 – 9:8).*

Whatever your reaction(s) to the grief you suffer, I desire that you do *not* grieve in vain. Remember, you are not a mismatch – or a misfit. My prayer is that the griefs you encounter summon you to a place of critical *reflection, re-appraisal, re-evaluation* and *re-dedication* of the meaning of your life to the very Owner of life, God, with such intensity and passion! This is one huge advantage the grieving experience affords us all without an exemption!

Appropriate Grieving and Mourning

How long is appropriate for anyone to grieve or mourn?

Wasn't that the same similitude of question God had asked Prophet Samuel when he had continued to excessively grieve for King Saul's spiritual backsliding and God's rejection of him as king of Israel *(1 Samuel 16:1)*.

While I may not be able to categorically recommend how long or short a period is advisable for grieving and mourning, there are examples of appropriate grieving and mourning found in the Bible. Being able to consider the reactions of the following few bereaved people at their losses of loved ones, colleagues and mentors should give you a clue:

- ***At Israel's death in Egypt:***

  When Israel or Jacob, the father of Prime Minister Joseph had died in Egypt at the ripe old age of 147, Egypt's parliament had according to their culture declared seventy days of national mourning in his honor! Thereafter, everyone had returned to work. But for Joseph – and his household – their mourning had been accompanied *"with a great and very sore lamentation"* which had lasted seven days.[1]

- ***At Prophet Samuel's death:***

  When Prophet Samuel had passed on, his protégé, the young David had departed for a more secluded place, in the desert of Paran to mourn his mentor's transition. *He had remained in a state of utter brokenness of heart, for just a while.* There had been a hot, deadly, pursuing assailant who had wanted to snatch his life, from whom he had had to continue to flee while he'd continued to train and enhance his weak 600-man army unto strength and tactical prowess![2]

- ***At the death of baby born to David and Bathsheba's adulterous affair:***

King David had had an adulterous affair with beautiful Mrs. Bathsheba Uriah – and had subsequently murdered Officer Uriah. When the baby had been born to them, Prophet Nathan had been sent of God to confront the king of his displeasure with his unscrupulous act, details of which not many people in the kingdom had knowledge of! Consequently, the baby had taken grievously ill. David had fasted and besought God's face for seven days, for the restoration of health unto the baby. But no; he had died.

As soon as *"David saw his servants whispered,"* the Bible says, he perceived that the child was dead! That was on the same seventh day. His next line of actions would baffle you:

> *"Then David arose from the earth, and washed, and anointed himself, and changed his apparel, and came into the house of the LORD, and worshipped: then he came into his own house; and when he required, they set bread before him, and he did eat"*

> — 2 SAMUEL 12:20

- ***When Elisha had lost his mentor to Heavenly chariots of fire:***

Prophet Elisha had become a bit irate the morning after he'd witnessed his mentor Elijah had been taken to heaven in a fiery angelic chariot. He had bitterly cursed a band of irresponsible men who had taunted him: *'Go up, Baldie; you're bereft of your master, Elijah.'*[3]

But notice, the aggrieved younger prophet hadn't stayed irritable for too long. We were told he had gone further from that irate incident onto Mount Carmel – from where he had started appropriating the anointing upon his master by a verifiable tangible double portion![4]

- ***When Jesus had learned of Herod's beheading of John the Baptist:***

Did you remember our Lord Jesus Christ's reactions at His knowledge of the ruthless beheading of his cousin and fore-runner, the renowned John the Baptist by the ruthless king Herod? The Master had withdrawn by a boat right into the seclusion of private isolation for a while before the throngs had found him.[5]

When He had resumed *work*, He had taught and fed the 5 000. St. Matthew recorded that after these had happened, Jesus He had departed alone, withdrawing further still onto the mountains, until the dawn of the next morning *(Matthew 14:13; 23)*. You too may request more time off work, should you indeed need to, until the dawning of new strength!

When the reality check of life hits, no fewer expected reactions than those mentioned above should be expected. The bereaved have an uncontested right to grieve and mourn. When my family had lost our elder sister Joan in 1982 at age 22, I had taken it most personally: I had been devastated. I was only 14. My emotional turmoil had stemmed from my anguish that the Lord had not revealed Joan's destiny to me previously as He had on many other incidents before their occurrences, so that appropriate spiritual measures could have been taken! That had been the thoughts in my young, inexperienced mind. As a boy-prophet like Samuel, I had had quite a few visitations from the Lord that I could confidently say today, in retrospect, far outweighed my knowledge and depth of the Word at that time. A little over three decades after losing my beloved sister, I can confidently proclaim upon the rooftops that God owes *not* any of us the prerogative to reveal *every* detail in this life to us before their actual occurrence. That is why He remains Sovereign – and we, the worthy candidates of His graciousness.

But I had been irate at God. In my foolishness, I had sulked and become surfeited by grief. I had stopped attending the christian fellowship and church services altogether for a period of four years. I had mourned and wept for just seven days but those were just enough number of days to have had both my tear-ducts run dry. I say it all the time that only recently in the past decade or so had the Lord begun restorative works within me that had re-enabled me to empathize with wet eyes again! Funny however, throughout those days of backsliding: July 1982 until September 1986, God had retained His ability within me to still be able to pray in the Holy Spirit with my heavenly language. How unfathomable is His love!

Are you mourning or grieving today? Be encouraged. Comforter Jesus is near. His Holy Spirit is still at work, albeit, silently. Possibly *very* silently!

If a friend of yours is grieving or mourning, a kind gift from you to them – if actually not the best – is your gift of respecting their individuality! If you are the one grieving today – or mourning the loss of a dear one or thing, permit me to quickly share with you succinct, relevant pieces of advice vis-à-vis:

1. ***Come to terms with your loss as a reality:***

    You're *not* having a dream. It has happened – and it *has* happened. Come to terms with your loss as a reality.

2. ***Embrace your person:***

    Embrace your person. Do *not* blame yourself for what you could have done – but did not do – to prevent the uneventful occurrence from happening! Remember the Bible teaches no misfortune could have penetrated a stronghold without the Lord's foreknowledge of its occurrence.[6]

3. *Switch to the 'privacy-mode' should you desire it:*

I have advised you to be an individual – and not a person kowtowing under the influence of pressure or peers. You will heal quicker *only if* you will allow yourself more time to be alone with *you* – and *your* feelings.

Would you be embarrassed at being with *you*? Switch to the 'privacy-mode' should you desire to!

4. *Let your feelings out:*

Letting your feelings flow freely is nature's way of getting rid of hitherto toxic chemical-imbalances that may accompany grief and mourning. Do not contain or bottle them up, within. Doing so could become costly to your health!

Job of old had grieved and mourned his predicaments in absolute silence for just seven days.[7] Jewish rites had it that a mourner reserved the prerogative to remain silent for as long as he grieved – and no comforter may be able to say a word until he had first opened his mouth to utter the first set of words. Job's observance of *not* spilling the bile and gall had, I believe, preserved him from falling into Satan's presumptuous trap of an untimely death! He had regained a double portion of what he hitherto had lost *(Job 42:10-17)*.

5. *Grieve. Mourn. Weep:*

Remember, "Grieve appropriately!" That's the summary of all I have been communicating with you the past eight pages.

6. *Get Outdoorsy:*

If you could afford the pleasure of observing time walking in the open serene countryside early in the morning or in the quieter evening hours, that *would* be therapeutic. Observe nature. Sit, watch and listen to the caressing noise the meandering river-currents produce in the summer. Listen to the birds chirp as the squirrels gather conkers in the *fall*. Sit under the canopy of a heaven lit by twinkling stars and far distant planetary bodies. Do *not* resign to life. Do *not* shut yourself in, away from God's beautiful nature: Get Outdoorsy. Observe a walk in the countryside. You're *not* a mismatch!

7. *Listen to classical music:*

The music of the great masters of the string-and pipe-instruments have been scientifically proven to soothe – and heal aching hearts and souls. Google such pieces by such names as Mozart, Beethoven, Bach, Handel, Tchaikovsky, Vivaldi, J.S. Strauss, Verdi and Choplin to name just a few. Invest in their CD's. Book to attend the re-performances of those historic pieces. Get listening; get living: *"If music is the food of love, play it on."*[8]

8. ***Surround yourself with people who would encourage you on the path to wholeness and soundness again:***

    For some, there are always going to be standby 'handy', Godly family members, colleagues and friends who have your sole interest at heart. Some others may not have the support and encouragement of such closely-knit family members and friends available to them. These should put in the efforts to surround themselves with well-wishers who would avail them their unflinching support to nurse their spirit back to wholeness and wellness again!

    They who may require additional help of professional counselors, ensure that you avail yourselves to Holy Spirit-filled-and-led counselors or ministers with proven integrity. Doubtless, you would likely be emotionally vulnerable during the spell of your grieving or mourning. That is *the* cogent reason you must endeavor to enlist the services of a true servant of God who would *not* take advantage of you!

9. ***Lastly, take time out to call upon God as Jesus had done:***

    If you follow the simple guidelines I have outlined above, irrespective of the type of grief you may encounter, I am positively convinced that you should doubtless emerge on the positive mend.

    Appropriate grieving isn't shameful. *You are not a mismatch* for mourning your loss!

In the next chapter, I would like to focus upon the term "midlife crises" in both men and women – and what could be done to ameliorate, alleviate and combat it, generally.

Chapter 4

The Unevenness of Mid-life Crises in the Sexes

"I have chosen to be happy because it is good for my health!"

— Voltaire

Even though the term "midlife crises" is nowhere found in the bible, nevertheless, it had existed in both sexes – even in biblical times! In my earlier book *'Destroying the Power of DELAY: Possessing Your Canaan'*, I had deliberately limited myself to addressing mid-life crisis in males only for reasons solely pertinent to the issues being discussed therein! But here, I shall avail you the instrumentality of familiarity of what transpires between both the female and the male sexes *if* they encounter this likely turbulence in life's flightpath!

July 3, 2013; Radhika Sanghani, a reporter for *The Telegraph*, a British newspaper wrote on the signs of mid-life crisis. She titled her article: *'Top 40 Signs of A Midlife Crisis Revealed.'*

Here's how she had lined up her findings. Read or pore through her list – and decide whether to have a laugh or become serious, just for once! According to Radhika, you are meant to be exhibiting midlife crisis signs if you could identify with just *one* of these *Top 40 Signs of A Midlife Crisis Revealed:*

1. *"Desiring a simpler life.*

2. *Still going to music festivals like Glastonbury.*

3. *Start looking up old boyfriends or girlfriends on Facebook.*

4. *Realise you will never be able to pay off your mortgage.*

5. *Joining Twitter so your bosses think you 'get' digital.*

6. *Excessively reminisce about your childhood.*

7. *Take no pleasure in your friends' successes.*

8. *Splashing out on an expensive bicycle.*

9. *Sudden desire to play an instrument.*

10. *Fret over thinning hair.*

11. *Take up a new hobby.*

12. *Want to make the world a better place.*

13. *Longingly look at old pictures of yourself.*

14. *Dread calls at unexpected times from your parents (fearing the worst).*

15. *Go to reunion tours of your favourite bands from the '70s and '80s.*

16. *Switch from Radio 2 to Indie stations like 6 Music.*

17. *Revisit holiday destinations you went to as a child.*

18. *Cannot envisage a time when you will be able to afford to retire.*

19. *Read obituaries in the newspapers with far greater interest — and always check how people die.*

20. *Obsessively compare your appearance with others the same age.*

21. *Start dyeing your hair when it goes grey.*

22. *Stop telling people your age.*

23. *Dream about being able to quit work but know that you'll just never be able to afford to.*

24. *Start taking vitamin pills.*

25. *Worry about being worse off in your retirement than your parents.*

26. *Want to change your friends but don't meet anyone new that you like.*

27. *Think about quitting your job and buying a Bed & Breakfast or a pub.*

28. *Flirt embarrassingly with people 20 years your junior.*

29. *Look up your medical symptoms on the internet.*

30. *Start thinking about going to church but never act on it.*

31. *Always note when politicians or business leaders are younger than you.*

32. *Contemplate having a hair transplant or plastic surgery.*

33. *Take out a direct debit for a charity.*

34. *Can't sleep because of work worries.*

35. *Hangovers get worse and last more than a day on occasions.*

36. *Constantly compare your career success with your friends.*

37. *Worry about a younger person taking your job.*

38. *Take up triathlons or another extreme sport.*

39. *Find that you are very easily distracted.*

40. *Realize that the only time you read books is when you are on holiday."*

More seriously, *not* everyone will experience midlife crisis in their mid-years. Some will collide with it fairly early like young David had.

David, was a product of illicit mixed paternal Jewish seed of Jesse and an un-named Moabite lady. He was the youngest of an unruly family of six older step-brothers who had outcast him from the family home. Because of God's unfavorable pronouncement on the country of Moab – alongside five other wicked tribes for their parts in suffering His children the Israelites during their exodus *en-route* the desert to Canaan – no Israelite may have any marital or sexual relations with any of those six tribes. Product(s) of such relationships were disregarded, dis-inherited and discounted. In other words, the society at large deemed such women and their offspring as legal misfits, miscreants or mismatches.[1] David had fallen short under that categorization. His family had coldly, brutally rejected him. Realities of such emotional anguish sparked by cold rejection had triggered off the young boy's advent with crises as early as before he had reached age 12.

An early sufferer like David apart, some conversely, incredibly enough may never experience "midlife crises." Yet, for the majority, midlife crises will reveal its narrow, oblong face somewhere around their midlife years. In other words, you may discover life slowing down somewhat when you're forty or forty-*ish* – or there-abouts. If that happens to be your experience at this season of life, you would do well to be re-assured that you're *not* alone. You are neither a misfit nor a mismatch – regardless of your race, ethnicity, nationality or gender!

Now, shall we examine the midlife crises in the sexes, starting first, with the female sex!

Midlife Crises in the Female Sex

To help me better aptly describe this topic – particularly the discomforting feelings associated with the female sex undergoing midlife crises – I accessed the writings of the editor at *Body & Soul* magazine, Australia, who seemed to have written extensively on the topic! Here are some excerpts of her submission and findings:

> *"A friend was recently made redundant from her high-flying job as a magazine editor. Now 39, this is the first time since she left school that she has not had a job. Unsurprisingly, it has hit her hard. Once confident and outgoing, she now struggles to get out of bed in the morning.*
>
> *Another friend, 44, who prioritised family over career, has, on the outside, an enviable life. But with both of her children now away at university, she doesn't quite know what to do with herself.*

'We call it a midlife crisis, but actually it can happen at any age, to any gender,' says Anne Devlin, a Sydney-based clinical psychologist.

So should we all expect a tumultuous shedding of the skin around middle age? And, rather than treating it as a negative experience and source of ridicule, could the midlife crisis be not only inevitable but a positive experience?

First, what does a female midlife crisis look like? Is it an addiction to Botox and plastic surgery in an attempt to turn back time? Or is it, like Eva Longoria's character in Desperate Housewives, having an affair with a teenager? Is it packing it all in and doing a Shirley Valentine?

For many, it may not be quite as dramatic. Less acute symptoms may be boredom, a feeling of worthlessness, loneliness and lack of meaning, depression and anxiety. Or drinking too much, repeatedly changing jobs or partners, or obsessively shopping but never quite finding the satisfaction you are looking for.

It could be triggered by divorce, a serious illness, redundancy, an empty nest, the loss of a parent. Or it can just occur out of the blue.

The important question is: why? What are the deep-rooted factors that cause many of us, between the ages of 35 and 55, to go through what can be a long, frightening and isolating transformation?

According to James Hollis, a psychoanalyst and author of 'The Middle Passage: From Misery To Meaning in Midlife' (Inner City Books), the midlife crisis is less a chronological event than a psychological experience.

He believes the first ripples can be felt in the late 20s. It is the end of what he calls the first adulthood. This means the end of the magical thinking that characterises childhood – "I am going to be an astronaut", "I'm going to be a famous singer" – basically, "I am immortal".

It is also the end of the heroic thinking of adolescence – "I'm not going to make the same mistakes as my parents" or "I'm going to write the Great Novel".

In the midlife crisis, we realise our childhood and adolescent dreams of immortality and specialness have been a bit of a fantasy. And this, essentially, is what a midlife crisis forces us to confront: the harsh realities of adult life.

No matter how much we compete with each other or how hard we try, we're all just the same. We can control nothing. We don't know what tomorrow will bring. It is a pretty major breakdown of all of our beliefs and assumptions. Biggest of all is the realisation we're all heading in the same direction, on a one-way ticket.

Devlin says the crisis happens when you begin to feel

that who you are is defined by society, by an external force over which you have no control. "It's basically an identity crisis."

Hollis believes that one of the most powerful shocks of midlife is the collapse of our tacit agreement with the universe. We grow up assuming that if we follow the rules, do as we're told, are of good heart, then everything will work out and we'll all live happily ever after.

It's usually at midlife that we realise life is not that simple. We realise bad things happen to good people and vice versa. Although this sounds grim, it can be incredibly liberating. It can force us to stop drifting. It can make us think carefully about the choices we make, their impact on others and what we want to do with the rest of our journey.

We live in an insanely competitive, materialistic, individualistic world – one that worships money, possessions, perfection and celebrity, and never lets us take a step off the treadmill.

Devlin feels that this is particularly true for women. "There is so much pressure on women to look beautiful and young. You're measured by what you look like, not by what's inside."

A midlife crisis is undeniably painful and can be destructive, but it can also serve as a vital wake-up call, particularly for women. According to research, the most profound difference in attitude between men and women going through middle age is that women are twice as likely to be hopeful about the future."[2]

Furthermore, midlife crises respect *not*, human gender, status or affluence. A highly placed woman married to a successful surgeon both of who were involved in a well-to-do christian ministry suddenly began contemplating a sudden 'flight of escape', without any reasonable reason. When asked in counseling what had led her that way of thought, she gave one quick answer: *"My unbridled emotional fantasies to just walk away!"* It had later emerged her father had walked away on both her mother and three younger brothers when she was younger!

Some individuals, based upon their genetic-components may suddenly, after a certain age begin to realize their inability to cope with the demands of living, generally! They may feel resentful at being a wife, a husband – or a parent. Some folk after undergoing series of life's troubles – including but not limited to grieving – may never be able to cope with the mental demands of their professed training.

Some women's midlife crises begin just after having a joyous baby. I might not be able to delve deeper into the various somatic-nervous-muscle-control ailments or the psychosomatic, psychological and emotional disorders relevant to crises generally; I am however quite optimistic that there are various medical names for each of these symptoms described. I should be most glad if you would prayerfully consult with a Holy Spirit-filled counselor – or medical expert who is competent enough to offer you both *diagnosis* and *prognosis*.

Moreover, someone at a diner outing may have become irritated over mere trifle in the way it was served! They have flared up. They could have been enraged over an unrelated pretty little petty disagreement with a loved one. The chemical imbalances in their brain-cells may be held to question; they may have suddenly become unstable in their moods – a stranger in a jiffy!

Another possible cause of a midlife crisis in the female sex has been described as the selfish narcissistic implosion in her mind to remain youthful-looking so much that she may find herself wanting to look younger, associate and form relationships with people as young as her own children! Or half as young as her age!

Whether it's an unexpected illness caused by a genetic bequeathal, a divorce or an empty nest; a psychological disequilibrium / neurological imbalance – or indeed, a deficit that has triggered the midlife crises you are experiencing, just remember, *you are not a mismatch*. God's grace will help you overcome – if you're willing to accept that grace!

As you begin to grasp the weight of growing older with wisdom, so also comes the realization of 'self-acceptance' that precedes a healthy balanced living! It could be a call from within!

Midlife Crises in the Male Sex

Midlife crises in the male may arrive at different times and seasons of their lives. It could hit a susceptible man who is in his early years – as early as in his 20's as I have been able to depict. Overall, studies show that midlife crises may be more associated with a psychological experience more than a series of chronological events. When at 38 I'd woken up one day to suddenly begin to discover that the hairs at my crown were thinning out, I had come to realize that I'd begun to readily mature with grace!

Like the female Aussie editor whose work I have quoted earlier had stated, a male top executive may find himself suddenly made redundant – or out of work. He would have to re-strategize. The truth is, he may not be able to respond to that state of shock, fast enough. He probably could be swept under, by the tides of depression feelings.

Some men may wrongly react to the adversity of this season of their lives by growing distasteful of what "would have", "could have" and "should have". One of the "should have's" in the lives of a couple past child-bearing ages is that deepening, enriching vital intimacy that should be deepening between them. For reasons best known to him and his psychological make-up, the male may suddenly begin to get tempted to withdraw emotionally, physically and financially from his wife of over three decades. Ironically though, he may at the same crises time begin to nurse the thoughts of (and indeed flourish in) a strange, strong appetite for a younger woman, if quick care is not taken!

Synopsis of David's Midlife Crises

Let's cast a quick look again at young David in the Bible. A string of events had led to the different crises-stages of his life! As earlier identified, his predicament had stemmed from his illegitimate birth as a half-Moabite. Soon, he had been outcast, shepherding a few sheep, back of the desert. Then he'd delved deeper into the unseen God – and had emerged fully possessed by extra-ordinary qualities none of his six half-brothers had dared to own: the anointing of God's Spirit! Then he had infiltrated the demoralized Israeli army and had accepted the challenge head-on, to confront defiant Goliath. He had slain Goliath at age fourteen – and the pretty young ladies had sung his praises, to the consternation of the king, Saul. Now, because of the king's insecurity, envy and outrage at the young warrior, David – even though had been destined to inherit the throne of Israel – had begun to hide in caves, skip around the bare, rugged terrains of the wilderness like a skilled lunatic-rockgoat. He had had to scheme his escape flightpaths away from the annihilative threats of Saul for about twelve years! For us fellow-inhabitants of today's modern microwave world, that could have translated to mean more than half a century spent on the run! In this fugitive state of existence, coupled with anxiety, anger, loneliness, frustration – and a concocted, less-than-stable-state of-mind, David would encounter the unimaginable duo of Mr. and Mrs. Nabal!

We should understudy both the inter-connectivity

between the rich and the poor; the affluent and the not-so-affluent in this story recorded for us, engaging the interactions that had ensued between the runaway guerrilla-leader-warrior and the duo of the affluent and powerful couple, Nabal and Abigail.

To forewarn you, a quick lesson needing being safely tucked away at the back of your mind is *your* mindfulness to not add to the torture of the broken! The afflicted is probably undergoing enough humiliation, bereavement, defeat and loss. Ubiquitous circumstances that usually surround the strange, sad, unpredictable occurrences involving midlife crises are taunting enough! If you could *not* mend the broken, please desist from adding to their injury! Flaunt my advice and you would have violated one of God's finest rules in the universe: *the right to privacy* and *the protection of human sense of dignity!* My counter-advice, Sir Nabal would exactly heed!

In *Chapter 5*, we shall encounter the Nabals – and David, the growing guerrilla leader.

Chapter 5*

An Unevenly-matched Married Couple Nabal & Abigail

"And there was a man in Maon, whose possessions were in Carmel; And the man was very great, and he had three thousand sheep, and a thousand goats: and he was shearing his sheep in Carmel.

Now the name of the man was Nabal; and the name of his wife Abigail: and she was a woman of good understanding, and of a beautiful countenance; but the man was churlish and evil in his doings; and he was of the house of Caleb."

— I SAMUEL 25:2-3

Major life decisions presented to us during or in the middle of life's crises must be approached with utter carefulness and wisdom, not flippantly! Nabal may have been undergoing a midlife crisis: for all I know, every finger points to the presence of symptoms of a man who was in dire crises despite his huge wealth! Remember again, midlife crises respect *not*, human gender, status or affluence!

A Quick Glance at Nabal

Nabal's name meant *"a fool"*; Abigail's, *"the joy of a father."* He was a direct descendant of Caleb – the same Caleb and Joshua team. In fact, Nabal had inherited Caleb's Estates of Maon and Carmel situated near Hebron. This was his main source of wealth. It was easier to multiply sheep, oxen and goats once the issue of the meadows had been established for all time. Sir Nabal possessed gigantic business acumen though he was a midget in godly virtues!

Hence, my question: *"Who really is rich?"* Is it he / she who is:

- Rich in goods and not God;

- Rich in God and not goods;

- Rich in goods and in gods, or;

- Rich in God and goods?

I believe firmly you have rightly picked the correct option![2] Not only was Nabal *poor* toward God, he was of poor manners. The Bible describes him as *"churlish."*

That word translates: *"a grunt, like a pig."* He was surly, snappish and always snarling like a dog. More, he was proud, loud and rude. Summarily, Nabal *"was rough and evil in his doings."*[3]

As I am yet to meet any who was bitter on the inside and had escaped the harrowing furrows of facial wrinkles; Nabal, I presume must have ploughed long ridges on his forehead: a very ugly man indeed! Ugly but rich. This was the man Abigail had been inextricably joined unto, in an everlasting wedlock.

A Quick Glance at Abigail

You would reckon Abigail to be Nabal's match. But, no! Quite to the contrary, Abigail was a ravishing beaut! She was a very pleasant lady *"of a beautiful countenance."*[4] I have attended many a wedding ceremony and have heard peoples' comments of the like: *"How did she manage to win the guy's heart?"* Or *"What on earth did she find attractive in him?"*

Physical beauty apart, Abigail possessed inner beauties. This is she whom the Bible commends searching, eligible bachelor-suitors to acutely target: an inner beauty, be-decked in an ornament of a meek and quiet spirit, which in the sight of God is of an inestimable price.[5]

Not only was Abigail physically and spiritually attractive, she *"was a woman of good understanding."*[6] When you possess understanding of a thing, it means you possess the ability to know *"how to"* successfully approach the diverse, wide-ranging issues that may arise on that subject. If you have understanding of the mechanics of life, for instance, it would suggest beyond an iota of a doubt, your wisdom to be able to successfully handle life's curved ball throws not limited to you, but including those of your spouse and children! You possibly cannot extricate *'understanding'* away from a full possession first, of the Holy Spirit of God and the Word of God. The *"spirit of understanding"* is one of the inseparable seven-fold spirits of the LORD found in *Isaiah 11:2* –

> *"And the spirit of the LORD shall rest upon him, the spirit of wisdom and understanding, the spirit of counsel and might, the spirit of knowledge and of the fear of the LORD."*

Now, if *knowledge* concerns *knowing* and *wisdom* pertains to *doing* what is known, then an *understanding mind* would imply a mind that is assured of the certainty of the outcome of knowledge applied to solve a problem.

> *An understanding mind comes with the unshakeable conviction that God will remain faithful to His word to bring to fruition any seed of a declaration made by Him!*

I know the next question agitating your mind: "If Abigail knew the Lord, and was a woman of understanding; why did she marry a fool – as glaring a fool, as Nabal?" Well, the most plausible reasons why Abigail had married Nabal might have included – but certainly not restricted to – the following:

1. Abigail as at the time of her wedding may not have been as spiritually matured as she had later become in latter years;

2. She could have been deluded by the endearing effects of Nabal's riches during courtship;

3. Poor Abigail may have been forcefully married to Nabal by a father who had an eye on Nabal's vast riches. (Worse could it have been if the arranged marriage deal had been sealed by her mother who may have been hell-bent on ensuring her futuristic financial security against old age at the sacrifice of her daughter's soul); or finally,

4. Abigail had deliberately compromised and laid aside the Spirit's restraints of red flags in courtship or engagement, blinded by love!

I am assured any of the conditions above could have been the case in those days as could possibly be, today! Because the Bible remains silent on reasons why Abigail had agreed to marry Nabal, no one may be able to accurately offer any particular clues! What I do understand is the Lord's unwavering commitment unto us as our Shepherd, to stand by us even in times of deep sorrow and regrets. Quite unfortunately though, Abigail eventually legally became Mrs. Abigail Nabal. In no sooner time, she probably would begin to grow tired and weary of such a mismatched union of drain and pain! Nabal on the other was a brute; he could not have cared more!

Wisdom Handling Situations Involving Inextricable Relationships

Like Abigail, David's marriage to Michal, King Saul's daughter had been pretty fixed. It had been arranged to the *tee* under the most bizarre of circumstances. Remember, King Saul himself had been experiencing tremendous pressures of midlife crises! The distressed king had announced three special reward pay-packets to anyone who could take Goliath down at the expense of his daughter's heart – among two others. The other two conditions involved: a sumptuous financial settlement and a waiver of his tax burden – and that of his family's to the kingdom![7]

You tell me what father does that?

Brave, anointed, handsome young David had found fame but fortune! Being of a humble, discounted background, he hadn't been up to the beat of suddenly becoming the king's son-in-law! King Saul, the wicked, opportunist father-in-law however, had no sooner than David's victory over Goliath quickly figured out how he would get rid of his son-in-law! He had conceived of a deft move: *use* his daughter's marriage and 'in-love' experience as a bait to entrap him. He had named Michal's dowry due him from David at just a mere one-hundred

Philistine foreskins. That way, the straddling young man would be no more. So he had thought in his evil genius and un-renewed mind! However, the Bible records that David *"behaved himself wisely in all his ways; and the LORD was with him."*[8] Saul had made a huge gaffe, again! David had laid at the king's feet, double his asking price! *If you were Saul, tell, what gutted reaction would have greeted you at the sight of David's feat?*

Read it for yourself: *"And Saul saw and knew that the LORD was with David"*; and became yet *"more afraid of David; and Saul became David's enemy continually."*[9]

In a short while, Michal, Saul's daughter had begun throwing tantrums in a blatant display of the *spirit of despise* against her husband – much like her father, the king had done. David however had demonstrated the "spirit of understanding." He'd tucked his hands into those very hands that govern the universe. He'd danced and rejoiced in the God of his salvation! Michal, however, had become accursed – and had died childless. She had been the only known woman in the entire scriptures who had perished un-regenerative![10]

Gaining Understanding about Inextricable Mismatched Relationships

Let me offer you practical insight with which you will overcome the less-than-desirable situation you find yourself, particularly, if you are involved in an inextricable, mismatched relationship:

- ***First, being in a covenant relationship simply means you're bonded:***

  If in a marriage situation, you'd be gladly told by the Groom's men: *"Boy, you're wedlock-ed!"* What your rejoiceful group of friends means is simply: you are bound both by an oath and a covenant agreement from which you may *not* be expected to seek dissolution.

- ***Second, if your relationship begins to deteriorate, you should not automatically abandon it any more than you do, a poorly child:***

  Instead of abandoning ship, *you* take care of that marriage. Most marital woes could be averted by a mere, down-to-earth, back-to-the-basics, one-to-one personal communication and dialog. Not assumptions.

  Now, if they refuse to engage in personal dialog, then, possibly communication with a respectable, Holy Spirit-filled counselor would do. Absconding from, abandoning home or absenteeism away from a spouse, days, weeks – or months on end on a purported overseas business trip or national back-to-back road trips would eventually spell doom for your marriage!

- ***Third, seek intermediation and counsel before trouble time!***

  You must not await the onslaught of confusion

time in your marriage before you had engaged Spirit-filled counselors to speak with. Truth is, both parties ought to have one – and not more than two – jointly, mutually trusted and respected, trained, relationship-marriage counselor or pastor they both can approach. Make these godly folk your trusted friends. Talk with them at length from time to time even when everything is seemingly okay between you and your spouse. Don't wait to spot a fox in your yard before you had erected your fences, high enough against an intruder. Unfortunately, many young couples are so guilty of the negligence of *not* engaging enough spiritual watchful eyes on the towers of their marriages – and relationships.

If you have waited for the tap-rooted dockleaf weeds to make intrusive appearances in your garden before you have acted, it's never too late to begin the arduous task uprooting! Doubtless, the process of uprooting is very laborious – but it is one for which you'll always be grateful. Uprooting is the only means of finally eradicating the dockleaf from your garden.

In the same vein, there is no grass greener on the other side of the fence. If it looks greener, it would still require some good, lawn-mowing skills of an expert gardener. Be *your* expert gardener!

- **Fourth, shadow elderly martially successful couples:**
There's a rich pot of wisdom in arranging time and again, opportunities to 'shadow' martially successful

older couples in your church whose marriages have spanned decades.

To *'shadow'* means to "come close to", "watch intently and closely", "stay with for a short time-period and ask pertinent questions" that relate to the secret of their loving relationship or that pertains to the hard-knot issues you currently are experiencing in your marriage. More wisdom is derived by your *shadowing* mature couples because you're offered genuine, unrehearsed conversation as they live out their lives in the glare of a fifth pair of eyes. More, *shadowing* leaves no room for second-guessing each other's reactions. Joyous, successful couples are also most grateful to share their lives with the younger ones, passing onto them the very recipes for the evident success in their own marriages.

If you're un-churched, call for some 'back-to-the-basics', trusted, elderly couple who knew you from your childhood days who would be happy to *not* mince words with you. Do *not* extend your plea of help to your biological parents who may be biased against your spouse, or they who would sing your praise telling you only what your ears would love to hear!

As I bring this chapter to a close, let me categorically emphasize that whenever a party defaults in covenant matters, the defaulter automatically brings a reproach on the less guilty. You may wonder at my conjecture of what incalculable loss the captain and the merchants had incurred on that Spain-bound merchant vessel Jonah had sneaked aboard on – alongside the fortuitous compensation sums the merchants' insurers must have parted ways with, at Jonah's unsolicited association!

Irrespective of the extent of your losses in a past irresponsible relationship that possibly had drained and left you divorced, shattered, bruised and broken; I declare unto you that you're not a misfit – neither are you a mismatch! Albeit, the *spirit of understanding* must be applied to all marital or relationship issues – at all times!

Demonstrating the 'Spirit of Understanding' in Troubled Relationships

Allow me to depict to you from Abigail's life, practical demonstrations of this phenomenon called the "spirit of understanding." I perfectly realize that we live in a fallen world – details of which are not hidden from God! Yet, with the exception of the biblical injunction mentioned by the Lord in *Matthew 19:9* – it is only upon the ground of infidelity; that is, marital unfaithfulness *could* a spouse instigate a divorce-case against the other. This personally speaking, does not mean a spouse could behave recklessly in their marriage and expect to go free. Severe attitudes that *should* lead to the death of any marriage should any spouse decide to engage in such include physical altercations, violations and aggravations. Other beastly attitudes that will necessarily suck you under the quicksands of marital woes are physical, mental, emotional and financial neglect and abuse, unreasonable behaviors up to but not limited to denying your spouse sexual intimacy (for a period up to but not pegged at six months); any abusive behavior, gambling, drunkenness, doping and drugging – and other conditions that may break, brutalize or lead to injury or threatening the life of your spouse and children! If any one of these grounds is cited by an afflicted spouse in a divorce or legal separation petition as ground(s) for seeking such legal separation or divorce, it shall be acceptable legitimate ground(s) for the dissolution of a marriage in most of today's divorce courts.

Ir-respective of whatever reason(s) a disagreeing, petitioning spouse has cited in a divorce petition, be aware of one resolute, unchanging, unequivocal truth stated by the Inventor of the marriage institution:

> *"For the LORD, the God of Israel saith that he hateth putting away: for one covereth violence with his garment, saith the LORD of hosts ..."*

> — MALACHI 2:16

If you do *not* believe the last couple of lines that God *hates* divorce, fine! All you need do is ask someone who has experienced one! By the way, never believe a couple of liars who try to mop over their misfortune and convince you otherwise, saying of their split as amicable. They shamefacedly lie: *"We had a jointly agreed amicable divorce."* It was either *their* marriage was based on falsity, or it was a staged marriage of convenience!

(Even in contracted marriages of convenience, we all know that God watches between the oaths and covenants exchanged. His word to hold both 'gaming' parties responsible still forever binds, regardless of the state of their criminal, hardened consciences!)

My point?

There had never been – and never will be – a divorce that ever was amicable. If the love was genuine and sincere within at least one of the parties, someone was bound to hurt – and hurt terribly! What about the un-imaginable hurt suffered by the children in particular, if children had been involved?

Your spouse may be terminally ill; would you reckon it in your understanding morally upright, to start seeing someone behind their back, whilst you pay them lip-served love?

If you are still confused about what direction your change of heart should take, be human enough, at least – and trade places with them. In other words, place yourself in your ill spouse's shoes. Be candid with your evaluation. Admit your conviction to your very self and God alone.

For Abigail, she did *not* abscond from *her* matrimonial home. Neither did she abandon *her* marital obligations to Nabal; she knew there had always been a just and true Judge above, Who had always vindicated every wrong. In the end, she had been correctly vindicated!

The *spirit of understanding* demands that you:

1. *Allow dusts to settle; dusts do settle down in the long run:*

Do not rush into marriage skipping the necessary period of courtship. That is essentially what the courtship period is meant for: the discovery of your intended mate within appreciable and healthy boundaries. This period of discovery – I would recommend should not be lesser than six months and may take up to two years, or slightly longer. It could take that long because an individual's willingness to "open-up" and avail themselves for discovery by another, varies from person to person.

I am flabbergasted by deep, spiritual men who claim God spoke to them about a sister in a vision of the night. Without first making attempts knowing her, they proceed to propose marriage to her. While a very significant few may have indeed been genuinely Spirit-led as such, majority have acted in a hasty human spirit of error. They have been gallantly proven wrong: the lady had been offended, her intelligence, insulted! These brothers have acted rashly and have lost what could have turned out to be great friendships – with potential for more! They have been wrong, you see; because they seemed to have forgotten that for a relationship to work, it must peacefully accommodate the co-existence of separate wills of two separate individuals from varying backgrounds, exposures and experiences of life!

For a rather different reason from the spiritual men mentioned above, I also do tend to not agree with ladies who claim both monopoly and superiority over the spirit of discernment; single ladies who claim they could *fully* "figure out" a prospective match by merely asking them questions on the phone. In many ways, their thought processes are just a replica of the "white-collar job interview" scenario – except again, the "politicians' TV debate" approach where prospective candidates slug it out with their rivals, each putting their best foot forward in order to win their party's nomination! We may both agree that the best candidate, sometimes, never gets the job through either means of vetting and choice! Both approaches are nothing short of gambles on personality-appeal contests to see who-best-ticks-the-box. That may be the way both western democracy and the *cosmos* are governed. Certainly, the way of worldly wisdom is at loggerheads with the way of Heavenly wisdom when it comes to a single lady choosing a marriage-mate *(James 3:13-17)*.

One more ill of the interview or debate approach to 'filtering' potential suitors is the hidden danger of making summative, hasty generalizations about them – either for the positive or the negative – just after a short while of getting to briefly acquaint with them via e-mailing and telephone conversation, particularly, if the relationship is long distant. Like the Sweet Psalmist of Israel had confessed, you may also someday – after a long while – have to sweetly own your fault:

"I had said in my haste, all men are liars."

— PSALM 116:11

You would soon realize that no two humans are exactly alike on the face of the earth. Your stereotyping the stream waded your canal-waterway is myopic and devoid of faith. All men and women are not the same as your *ex*; so stop making hasty generalizations about God's diverse creation of sizes, species, ethnicities, diversities, races, looks and shades of colors. If you let those genuinely sent of God slip through your long, slender fingers, in your moment of clarity of mind in latter months or years, you would come to agree with me that not everyone is dodgy.

One the other hand, possibly your mind has started playing you a game to accept everyone as they first appeared. That's yet another misrepresentation of the truth: people are never as real as they had first presented themselves at a first 'meet'. Someone who is serious on issues related to life and eternity just seem to get better, by the day; they do not stagnate. And that's where the clue to a balanced, successful courtship-approach is found: in the long run!

Trust you me: dusts do settle, in the long run!

If you would fully maximize the essence of a true courtship, you must be yourself – while allowing your mate to be themselves. Don't be uptight. Make them feel welcome. Never hastily assume you know anyone. Take notes of little things; little, almost insignificant things do always add up. Allow them to mirror their true semblance in the mirror of your genuine love.

Even if you discovered that you're not compatible with this saint after courting, and you have to discontinue the relationship, be human. Be kind. Be firm. Appreciate them for the chance to have met them. Do not abscond. Do not leave them guessing your decision. Do not string them along. If there are books, possessions, keys to locks and doors you must return, reach an agreement on how you would return them. Engagement rings should be honorably returned; do not speed off to pawn them. If they asked you to keep it, ask them to state it in a written form or in an email. Money loaned to you must be returned. Do not crush another's spirit. You will be blessed for your honesty, sincerity and integrity. Long story, short: I'm an advocate for a longer-than-six-month courtship, before marriage.

2. *During courtship, ensure you both submit to a final authority that will ultimately guard your code of acceptable conduct:*

For the born again child of God, our final authority

lies in *doing* the words *read* in the Bible, God's holy Word! This is our absolute, uncompromising standard. Now, if the person you're dating isn't interested in reading to discover and practise the Word with you in courtship, what on God's earth gives you the impression that they will suddenly 'grow' after you both are married?

Isn't that an obvious, flashing red flag, already?

3. ***Ensure you have trusted counselors, pastors and elders praying for you:***

The Bible says: *"Where no counsel is, the people fall: but in the multitude of counsellors, there is safety."*[11]

4. ***Ensure you do not resort to stonewalling or dealing the 'silent treatment':***

Resorting to a flight of silence, stonewalling or dealing the 'silent treatment' whenever you have an argument or a disagreement in courtship or marriage are sure signs of your emotional immaturity and selfishness. These convince me that you are a control freak. They point the hand at you as an emotional abuser.

Have you ever watched little children disagree, settle and make up after a disagreement? If you haven't, I challenge you to watch toddlers' 'fight' and 'make up' – across all cultures around the world! Like those peace-seeking toddlers, talk matters through

– attempting to sort them out between both of you, first. Schedule time to listen to each other – and hear each other well. Do not depart for your house (if you're courting) or go to bed (if you're already married) without having first settled the *issues* of the day. Choose to forgive – and make allowances for the occurrence of errors.

Do not tally your spouse's wrong-doings; you ain't no cop! Even at that, tough cops sometimes do relent, in their powers booking an offender!

5. **Keep all third parties out of your disagreements and matters:**

Your relationship is first and foremost between God, you and your spouse – or significant other. Imagine in your mind's eye, drawing a triangle with God, your spouse and you. God sits atop the triangle, your mate at bottom right and you, at the bottom left! That's a complete "marriage-tri-unity". Nothing more. Nothing less – and certainly, nothing else!

"Third parties" have a way of magnifying issues, diversifying opinions, interests and attention. "Third parties" are inclusive of your children / step-children; blood relatives from both sides – and closest friends, excluding your mutually trusted Spirit-filled counselor! I know you just felt like a sledge hammer tumbled onto your toe, particularly that I included both of your parents in the category of "third parties." You know, I had sworn before the Lord at my ordination to teach the complete truth of the Gospel – and nothing but the truth.

Leave your parents out of your marital matters. Simply make your spouse your *best* friend; the *first and only party*, after God!

6. *Never threaten to leave your spouse:*

I have earlier mentioned some signs of *the* emotional abuser. The baseline common denominator-indicator of *every* emotional abuser is their pathetic, uncanny ability to heave a heavy guilt-burden on the innocent partner. They play the victim – and make you feel grossly undeserving or sorry. Some spouses would actually begin to rant when just a little displeased. In their rants, they threaten to forsake and abandon their spouse. Your threats grossly point the accusing fore-finger at you as an emotional abuser in this relationship! Irrespective of who else you later met, you'd always take the old "you" with you. You've got some work to do on *you!*

Threatening to forsake your spouse is a gross form of emotional abuse. It demoralizes the spirit, builds distrust, anger, frustration and resentment in the abused spouse. It is a form of controlling and coercing a spouse, partner or significant other to conform to your whimsy-wishes. How pathetic; you must have sunk so low as to put on the conduct of a misfit – or a mismatch.

Marriage I.C.U or Divorce

1. ***If they did not threaten; but you must separate from them:***

   If they haven't a culture of calling the bluff to separate from you, but you have independently reached the sad conclusion that you need to offer this relationship or marriage a 'fallow' time because of unseen debilitating factors hidden from the public you have endured for years, spell out in no uncertain language, the reason(s) for your resolve. Express yourself in as easy-to-understand statement as: *"Darryl, I am leaving you because of your resolve to not undertake therapy to address your unreasonable behavior of an addiction to ______."* Name such irrational behavior they may be addicted to such as substance abuse, drinking, gambling away family's money, undue neglect, self-harm, violence and assault, refusal to use medication that poses a health-risk concern to them and you *etcetera*.

   You *must* remain firm, resolute and calm. Always have a second party with you for protection and need of witness whilst you leave, just in case trouble brews – as it usually could potentially do!

2. ***Now that they or you have left, you're now separated:***

   Now that they or your have left, you're now separated.

   What does that spell for either spouse?

First and foremost, your separation at this time is still *not* a legal separation. You're still legally married – and bitterly hurt. You must now jointly determine which direction to steer the marriage at this stage. A period of separation – whether legal or otherwise is an indication that your marriage is extremely poorly – and in a dire need of urgent attention, tender loving care and possibly, an *ICU*. Notice, a legally separated spouse is still a married spouse! Hence, dating another person at a crucial time when your existing marriage dithers between convalescence and a possible recovery from the Intensive Care Unit is ethically, morally, legally and spiritually wrong. It is called an affair! It is in order to not be labeled as adulterous that some will do anything to *kill* the existing marriage for a new flicker of love. We all undoubtedly recognize such as the real mismatches, misfits and miscreants!

3. *What to do while separated but not divorced:*

Your spouse may be in recovery; a rehabilitation home – or incarcerated! It is while separated but *not* divorced that the commonest weaknesses in either partner, like troubled dregs begin to brew in the teacup. So also do the seducers, tempters and temptresses: like rabbits, they, from nowhere start emerging from the forest's woodworks. It is obvious your marriage had kept those sneaky, jumpy, fidgety, crawly, beastly creatures at bay all while long!

In order not to be caught off guard, a partner may begin to forcefully self-reform with the ultimate goal of pushing for reconciliation with an estranged spouse, at all costs. While the female may struggle with her overwhelming emotions and become very heartbroken, the male in particular encounters hardship coping with strong feelings of guilt, shame, under-achievement and failure! He could be as overwhelmed as his estranged wife is even though he has chosen to rather internalize stuff and deliberately appear 'strong' on the outside! But you'd agree with me that a man that truly lacks vulnerability isn't a very handsome man. Even God says a broken and a contrite-spirited persona is irresistible to Him *(Psalms 51:17)*.

While seeking reconciliation should be the ultimate mutual goal of separated spouses, the timing may just *not* be perfect because the persistent ills, addictions or addictive behaviors that had lured them onto Separation Blvd., may not just have been completely healed from! This scenario is the resultant effect of either spouse who attempts to recover from the ills that had had them overpowered through sheer will-power! You would rather do well to request the help of God's Holy Spirit than trying hard to work stuff out in your will power. Any separated spouse who had primarily separated out of the frustration, sorrow and brokenness of living a defeated life – and not just for mundane, selfish, twisted or manipulative reasons – truly seeks *for* help!

Married people separate for many different reasons: some, out of acrimony; others, to protect themselves and their children from addicted, angry, hate-filled, armed, dangerous, possibly violent and mentally-unstable spouses. I cannot be the judge of peoples' different motives. I may be able to reasonably suggest however, that records of the *offending spouse's* many attempts to become healed ought to be logged with their certified counselor. The *'offended spouse'* too should begin to lay hold upon the healings of their emotional state at this time, possibly through engagement with same counseling!

I am of the personal opinion that sexual relationship between hurting – and probably – warring, separated couple should *not* be happening just yet, simply because the core-motive why their marriage had slid into a convalescing state must *not* be forgotten neither abused! A lady's heart may begin to draw closer and crave deepening intimacy once again with an abusive-husband once sex beclouds her mind. The male, by virtue of his anatomy *could* gainfully employ sex as a means to an end because of his ability to de-compartmentalize sex away from true love! For the female; sex, her emotions and the desire to be loved may not be that so easily detached!

Both mates ought to be deeply seeking the face of God to touch and heal their hearts of hurts and pains at this time, rather pushing for physical intimacy which *should* indeed sabotage and short-circuit the entire healing process.

4. ***If you eventually get divorced, don't enter the rebound game:***

If you follow my elaborate piece of counsel in the preceding paragraphs, I guarantee you anywhere between 28 – 31% slim chance of witnessing your spouse's reunion with you in a stronger, healthier, marital commitment – and a tighter bond.

For any separated couple who successfully completes my suggested mandated routine of a godly counseling therapy prior to their re-union, I really would love to read from you. I'd be so glad to be associated with your triumph-of-love stories. Please write me to:

pulsepublishinghouse@harvestways.org

Conversely, if you did eventually proceed to get a divorce, I would be so sorry indeed, to learn of this painful development. But please do not rebound! Don't avail yourself for rebound games; emotional-rebounds are a sure way to loose and bleed again. Be not drowned by guilt-feelings, either! Again, seek both the comfort and the support of your trusted friends, families, pastor and Spirit-led counselor!

Reflect on the pathways you have trodden the entire period of your dead marriage: divorce had *never* resulted solely from the actions of just *a* spouse.

Your reflective moments will enable the Holy Spirit illuminate the dark recesses of your heart. Healing will follow His convicting power.

Observe *you-time!* Create time to pamper – and at times, indulge your passions. Remain pure in heart, though!

Ensure you're nurtured back to health before you consider getting emotionally entwined with another person, project or venture. Divorce does drain the *very* life of involved parties along with their finances regardless of how strong a personality each may be! Some other times, God's Spirit had re-joined the hearts of divorced couples many years after their divorces – having chosen to not remarry any other. He could repeat the same, for you.

5. ***Purchase – and read "Before You Step into Someone Else's Shoes":***

Without having to appear to make a merchandise of you, I would advise you to purchase – and read my book *"Before You Step into Someone Else's shoes,"* published by *PULSE Publishing House, U.K., 2010*; ISBN 978-0-9567298-0-4, before you decide to make another crucial life decision. I recommended it to you because of the feedback-reports I have received from across the world of the impact it has had upon the decision-making processes of those who have read it. An inexpensive, small, but powerful book (it's the cheapest of my written volumes), you would devour it in less than an hour. Order copies from *harvestways.org* today. Be healed spiritually, emotionally, psychologically, physically, financially and otherwise in the name of the Lord!

You are not a misfit – neither are you a mismatch!

* *Portions of this chapter have been culled, excerpted, re-written and adapted to suit the purposes of this book from 'DESTROYING the Power of Delay: Possessing Your Canaan'. Copyright; granted.*

Chapter 6*

Guarding Against Mismatched Sibling Rivalry Engendering Hatred

"Each child belongs to all of us and they will bring us a tomorrow in direct relation to the responsibility we have shown them."

— LATE DR. MAYA ANGELOU

Kindly permit me to send a shudder through your being. Here it is: If you are a God-*gem*, you are featured on the devil's nightly updated hit-target feed! *Did you read that?* Read it again, perhaps much more slowly: "If YOU are a GOD-*gem*, YOU are featured on the devil's hit-target list!"

Why would that be so?

The reason is not far-fetched: The devil always targets great potentials. His mindset is to have them sifted like the chaff of wheat before winnowing them in turbulent winds, to the end that they may *not* attain unto their destiny. But here's the *Goodnews*: if he failed to thwart Joseph's destiny, he will woefully fail in all his wicked machinations against you too, in Jesus' name!

"But as for you, ye thought evil against me ..."

— GENESIS 50:20

This dirty, sniper-fella *really* did plot against Joseph's destiny in every way – and at every turn. As Joseph overcame one hurdle after another – and attempted to turn the bend and gather momentum to pace the home stretch; over-sized, mismatched, unfair victimization-claims had hamstrung him at the Achilles'. His first crisis had showed up shortly before his twelfth birthday, by virtue of his brothers' hatred of his dream prowess! This would be the summation of the next foundational 17 years of his life, until *his day* had arrived. His *day* had ushered in God's blue-print design for his destiny. *May your due day also arrive.* We shall later see the various victimization-claims Joseph had endured. In the interim however, let us grasp a deeper understanding of the name, *Joseph*.

"Joseph" is a short, significant prayer; meaning: *"Let Him Add."* A more accurate rendition ought to be: *"Let God*

Add to Him." By this interpretation, we understand that young Joseph had a destiny to fulfill. He had the covenants, both of increase and preservation:

> *"But as for you, ye thought evil against me; but God meant it unto good, to bring to pass, as it is this day, to save much people alive."*

— GENESIS 50:20

A person's destiny is wrapped up in the expression of their given name. Though we were not told of when he had first had an encounter with God, we understand that he – and his family – had inherited the covenant of the God Who had introduced Himself as the *"God of Abraham, Isaac and Jacob."*[1]

Through his encounter with God, Joseph had realized with unshakeable understanding that God would someday make him great both as a deliverer – and a *savior*. Savior of his race! While his prosperous little heart had rejoiced at God's prime choice of him as a minister of His salvation, what information he may *not* have been de-briefed were the details of the invariably great pains he would undergo to emerge as such preserver of lives. *Isn't that exactly – with the exception of a few individuals – Heaven's modus operandi?*

Often in His majestic wisdom, God usually has revealed a large expanse of a glorious vision, in parts, until its complete fulfilment. Only Saul of Tarsus at his conversion experience and Baby Jesus Christ at His lowly birth would both be exceptions to this rule. Saul – who subsequently became Paul had had his crises summed up as revelatory at his calling on the Damascus road: *"for I will shew him how great things he must suffer for my name's sake."²* Jesus' crises, on the other hand, had been foretold through the prophets! God's old-time *seers* had by the Holy Spirit prophesied of the agonizing, full cup of God's wrath from which He must fully drink – its dregs notwithstanding – for the remission of the sins of the entire world!

Fiery Tests *En-Route*
Joseph's Destiny-fulfilment

Joseph's sudden rise to becoming the Prime Minister in Egypt was a poignant event. But it had taken a journey of 13 years detailing the daily bending, sculpturing and fashioning of an innocent young man's submissive will to fully obey God while His fiery flames had mercilessly purified him. The devil *tempts*. God *tests*. God's tests would include verifying whether or not Joseph's raw will, desire and choice-making process would succumb to lust in exchange of gaining sexual gratification, power – and possibly the spirit of bitterness that would have blighted his pure conscience, on one hand. On another hand, God's furnace fire had separated the dross from the gem; and had presented a totally purified, reflecting precious stone. The budding wise young man had *had* to choose between the silkier alternatives of savoring a life of indulgence and heading for God's excruciating, character-molding blocks! Joseph had consciously chosen wisely! Believe me, you and I are expected to make the same choice if we must significantly become God-inspired instruments of change in a rotten world!

Not only would Joseph be sore tested, his destiny-track would be spiritually engineered by variables completely outside his sphere of domain. He would henceforth become a victim until Providence would trump him victorious!

Shall we quickly consider some of the victimizations this untainted young God-*gem* had endured?

11 Unfair Victimizations of Joseph

1. ***Victim of Father Jacob's favoritism and transferred love:***

   Joseph was the eldest son of his father, Jacob's true love Rachel, who hitherto was long barren. Jacob's other wives: Leah – whom he had been deceived into marrying by his Uncle Laban – and Rachel's maids, Bilhah and Zilpah had borne him ten sons and a daughter before Joseph's arrival into the family scene. Very soon afterwards though, Rachel would pass away delivering Benjamin, Joseph's only sibling!

   Joseph, *"the son of Jacob's old age"* had become a half orphan. He had had the love Jacob had meant for

Rachel, his mum, transferred onto him.[3] It had been undeniably obvious: Papa had made *Jo*, a special *"coat of many colors"* which when his brothers had beheld had made them hate him all the more, very passionately. The Bible records: *"They hated him, and could not speak peaceably unto him."*[4] You've just read it; your preference of one child above the other(s) will pave the pathway for sibling-rivalry and passionate hatred among those children!

2. ***Victimized by loving an unruly, un-objective brotherhood:***

Joseph had grown up in what we could call a mixed / blended family setting (in today's western context), or a fierce polygamous setting (in the third world context). At any rate, his half-brothers were of the *wild caste* because the Bible attests in *Genesis 37:2* that they had conducted their affairs with a spice of notoriety and evil! The report Joseph had brought father Jacob had been his most candid capture of their nefarious activities on the field! He hadn't told a lie on them. He had been absolutely objective:

"… and Joseph brought unto his father their evil report."

Direct people always have had problems with biased, twisted, multi-choice, emotive, un-objective kind of people. Direct people never seem to know how to ascertain the degree of shades of the color grey contrasted on white and black; to them, colors are either white or black. Joseph lacked an ounce of diplomacy while preparing and filing his report to father Jacob! Whatever submission he had made – we know in retrospect – had been instigated by love, *not* hate!

3. ***A victim in reverse, of correctional mindedness:***

How often true it is that those whom we intend to correct and instruct in righteousness would soon begin to hate us? Young Joseph had the good of his brothers at the back of his mind when he'd filed a report with father Jacob. But he'd become a victim in reverse!

4. ***Victimized by his lack of emotional and psychological self-restraint:***

Joseph's dominant temperament could best be described as *'sanguine.'* This is the *"warm blooded, effervescent, bubbly, helpful, serviceable but chatterbox-personality-type of people."* Having many strong factors in their favor, one quickly traceable trait of weakness of people with dominant *sanguine* personality is that they tend to *over-react emotionally* or *talk without restraint* particularly when excited, until their mouths have landed them in a hot mess!

Could it be that Joseph's accurate report to father was unnecessary – and unwarranted?

Not necessarily!

Rather, I personally submit that Joseph had over-encumbered his brethren with his many words. And they *had* hated him!

He would however soon begin to learn to renew his mind in order to recreate whatever either had proceeded into his mouth – or out of it. There has never been *any* who had achieved the pinnacle of the destiny God called had ear-marked for them without first bridling their mind and tongue. (Other personality types are the *choleric*, *phlegmatic* and *melancholic.* Google these terms someday to learn more about each of them!)

5. *Lack of depth at controlling his spiritual gift:*

Being endowed with extraordinary spiritual gifts is *not* enough to see you to the top. A visionary must exercise his gifts with utmost discernment. The people, the time and the environment in which to share the heavenly vision require a *release* in the spirit. If you flagrantly flaunt my piece of advice, your dream will probably end up auctioned over a dinner of macaroni and spaghetti!

Once flashed onto the screen of your mind, the vision must be kept within your mind's decoding-monitoring device code-locked, until the season the safest opportunity to reveal it to the world arrives. Saul, revealed as Israel's king-elect through the mouth of Prophet Samuel would *not* in his sane mind divulge to his inquisitive Uncle, the prophecy of his proposed kingship.[5] If Saul's action here had earned God's recommendation, it must be worthy of emulation by all! Precocious

Joseph had exercised his spiritual gifting immaturely. He had found himself chained onto the auction blocks – sold off by his audience: *"And they hated him yet the more for his dreams, and for his words"* (Genesis 37:8).

While Joseph's brothers had scoffed, breathed out cruelty and conceived a mischief against their kin, father Jacob had *"observed"* his son's prophecies.[6] Jacob's strict observance ought to be the reaction also, of godly parents who would not serve as crisis-factors to their children's visions. Remember, Mary the mother of Jesus also had kept all of Jesus' *"sayings in her heart."*[7] Hence, it is a godly parenting-skill for parents / guardians to closely observe and monitor their children's *'sayings'* until those *'sayings'* become reality! And if your child / ward seems *not* to have any *'sayings'*, you go ahead and verbalize some *'sayings'* over them.

6. ***A victim of brothers' conflicting interest and conspiracy theories:***

"And when they saw him afar off, even before he came near unto them, they conspired against him to slay him."

— GENESIS 37:18

Their long-awaited day to "mess" with his destiny eventually arrived. Driven by rage, envy and age-long malice, they conspired to terminate his life. But God intervened, however, through the instrumentality of Reuben's counsel. He saved Joseph's life from their murderous plot. We applaud Ruben. Most of us thought his motives for performing this heroic salvation act were *very* laudable. Ah, not quite! Come with me.

Scripture declares in *Genesis 35:22* that Reuben had an incestuous relationship with Bilhah, the youngest of Jacob's wives! This wicked deed automatically waived off him, the rights of the first born son – which had entitled every first born male in the Jewish culture of that time, a double portion of his father's inheritance. Ruben had sinned against his own soul, his step-mother Bilhah – and against his father, Jacob. But wait; there still was one more person whose forgiveness he deeply craved. As this incestuous incontinence was committed after the death of Rachel, it wouldn't just be a crime against Jacob and Bilhah alone. It could be rightly regarded as an indirect affront well aimed at Joseph too, since Bilhah was logically, Joseph's step-mother! Hence, Bible scholars are *not* unmindful that Reuben's act of saving Joseph from the gallows had been an attempted showy piece of evidence of his external penitence for his earlier secret sins. A very shrewd *act*:

- Ruben inwardly coveted to have restored unto himself the first born rights and privileges. (Those rights and privileges, however, wouldn't ever be his or Judah's prerogative – but the righteous man sold as a slave to the Midianites);

- Ruben contrived, inwardly, to attempt to convince father Jacob with his supposed re-gained sense of responsibility, through his magnanimity towards Joseph: the evident proofs of this was the pit slime that had smeared his garments; and lastly,

- Ruben intended to have convinced Joseph of his support and love for him (which he genuinely did *not* possess), in order to have earned his forgiveness for violating his step-mother.

7. *A victim of brothers' cold rejection:*

The fear of rejection or neglect – particularly by loved ones and blood relations could become the root of mental agony and torture, depression, love-sickness, psychological traumas and various other dysfunctions – not forgetting, possibly, insanity.

Are you undergoing rejection – or know anyone experiencing the after-effects of rejection at this time?

Receive the comforting, re-assuring, healing love of God that *you are loved and highly valued* in Jesus' wonderful name.

Joseph's brothers' act of rejection was a sure clue of their cruel and murderous intents! Once they had thrown him into the pit, they had the peace in their mischievous little hearts to nurse their fleshly desires. The Bible categorically states that *"they sat down to eat bread."*[8] God's word teaches there is an inherent curse reserved for those who could afford dwelling at ease, in Zion. This interprets, God frowns at folk who are so apathetically indifferent to others' plights, having *"not grieved for the affliction of Joseph."*[9]

8. *Joseph was a victim of a "sell off":*

Before Reuben's return to the company later in the day, Joseph had been sold as a slave to the Ishmeelites. Take this: whenever anyone had initiated an action on behalf of a family or group – having *not* received an overall majority's authority to act on behalf of them, such action *should* never be bleached of error. Precocity is not an excuse for correctness! A couple of instances bear witness to this truth. First, king Saul had been judged to be in the wrong – and had lost his rulership the moment he had gored into the *priestly office* and offered a sacrifice unto the Lord on behalf of Prophet Samuel who deliberately had arrived late.[10] Second, Nadab and Abihu had been stricken dead at the altar, the embers of which they had stoked after offering a *"strange fire before the LORD."*[11] Nobody had mourned their demise!

Now, permit me to quip that the proceeds of any *'sell-off'* are the price of blood! Such proceeds cannot and must *not* be deemed as acceptable offerings before the altar of the living God! Proceeds from illicit sex, sex labor-camps, parlors and escort agencies; or the wages of prostitution, pole-dancing and pornography amongst the rest, the Bible refers to as the *"the hire of a whore"* and *"the price of a dog"* in *Deuteronomy 23:18.* Proceeds from these and such other questionable employment-types including but not limited to drug-supply or sale; politically looted public funds secretly lodged, laundered or stashed away from national auditors are *not* worthy offerings at the holy altar of God. Such accursed gifts are not worthy remunerative or endearing gifts to disciplined, holy servants of God, either! These are abominable gifts offered by abominable, cursed souls: society's proper misfits, mismatches and miscreants. Consequently, such as pollute and become polluted shall undoubtedly suffer the libation fire of He Who calls Himself: *"the Consuming fire."*[12]

'Sell–off' history is quite traceable in biblical history. In Prophet Joel's days, parents with a numb conscience had *'sold'* a daughter for a bottle of wine and pimped a son — if he was fortunate enough to have escaped being offered in a practical burnt offering to the monstrous horse-man god Molech.[13] Esau, Joseph's uncle had *'sold'* off his birthright to the better than he for a plate of porridge.[14] Judas, the betrayer, had *'sold'* Jesus Christ the Righteous One, for mere thirty pieces of silver! [15]

*Are you currently involved in a 'sell-off' deal of
a close friend or family member?*

You know, 'sell-off' deals do not always involve exchanging fiscal monetary proceeds. Whenever you have intentionally, wickedly ignored; neglected or deliberately "hands-off" the vulnerable as to open the door for evil to befall them, for example, you are guilty of not having discharged your moral duty to protect and preserve the powerless. The abductors, conductors, middle-men and women – including the end of the chain consumers of the abominable processes involved in both children and women-trafficking will not escape the fiery wrath and anger of God's judgment. You have sown the wind, you will reap the whirlwind *(Hoshea 8:7)*.

The young man Joseph had been 'sold off' to the slave-merchants for mere twenty pieces of silver via ordinary, hands-gesticulation, behind-the-hood-whispered-communication. This had been the base negotiable price his physique had fetched on that day! Some other day, he would further fetch the Ishmaelite merchants, a greater gain in another 'sell-off' to Potiphar!

And what do you opine Joseph's brothers had done with the proceeds of his sale?

Because they had been governed by the flesh, they possibly had eaten and gotten drunk. I imagine they probably had had a fight over apportioning the rest of the money after satisfying their lasciviousness. This had been why later in life they had been inevitably ravished by famine! Prophet's Jeremiah's words had haunted folk in his day who had dealt harshly with, tormented or shed the blood of an anointed innocent person:

> *"But know ye for certain, that if ye put me to death, ye shall surely bring innocent blood upon yourselves, and upon this city, and upon the inhabitants thereof …"*
>
> — JEREMIAH 26:15

Jesus' blood unjustly shed consigned the nation of Israel – up until this day – onto the dark period of their minds' alienation from a deeper understanding of the knowledge of God. This was that which Prophet Jeremiah had spoken of as the time of *"Jacob's trouble"* – though, ironically, this period would work together for good for the procurement of Gentiles' peace![16]

9.   *A victim of parental old age loneliness battle:*

Care-giving is a real major issue we should be more than ready to grapple with. We live in a system that is finding it increasingly tough to cater for our elderly citizens! So who should care for the elderly? The older citizenry certainly do *not* want to be a burden of any sort to the younger! But just as the thinning of the crown and temple hair-lines in men in their mid-years and the corresponding menopause and its flushes in the female in advancing years are naturally expected occurences; growing old must be embraced and accepted as another graceful, natural stage in the cycle we call *"life."*

I know some people who dread getting old. But I simply *cannot* wait to live old – or wait for you to grow old! I believe it is a blessing from the Lord to get to live old. Maybe you've heard me say I'm gunning for 120 years before I'd be ready to call it quits – that is, if the Lord permits me! Now, before my pen diverts, the question remains: *Who should cater for the elderly?*

First and foremost, the answer to this question lies with the elderly-to-be: that is, the virile, active aged *18-65 workforce group* of today. They can best begin to re-orientate their thought patterns of youthful years evidenced by their lifestyles, to reflect the kind of care *they* would love to receive when they become old. This is because the way we pattern to invest our youthful years inevitably, *should* set the precedent for our expectation of returns on how we spend our aged years. The key is found in one summative word: I–N–V–E–S–T!

Invest and plan for old age *now*, while you are young and able! Make strong efforts to invest where it matters. Invest in God – and the things of God. Invest in the people God has placed in your life: *your* spouse and child(ren) – if you have them!

"Each child belongs to all of us and they will bring us a tomorrow in direct relation to the responsibility we have shown them."

— LATE DR. MAYA ANGELOU

The influential people in our lives are the first, basic, rightful investments we all must endeavor to put strong efforts, investing into. If you're married, the very first personality worthy of all your love and affection after God, is your spouse! Then your children – or adopted children, if you have adopted any. Then your parent(s), before other relatives and friends. That should be the prioritized working hierarchy of your affection. Dare re-arrange this heaven-ordained *set-up* – and you should smell potential trouble!

Deny disagreements any opportunity to erect walls of partitioning between you and your loved ones! Always find a way to mend the bridges. Forgive, restore – and forgive again!

Your aged parents and relatives too have their special places in sharing your love and lives. You and your spouse would do well to agree to unbiased, balanced, common grounds upon which you will share your love–lives with them. Don't be selfish here: whatever is good for your parents must be exactly good for spouse's parents – or step-parents, it makes absolutely no difference.

Aged loved ones *may* become prone to loneliness – particularly if they have been active all their life! Loneliness cannot be cured with money, riches, lands or fame – except by the cherished companionship and love of other loved ones.

Joseph's father, Jacob was *not* a poor old guy. But by this time however, certain truths about becoming aged must have started to dawn on him. He allowed his emotions to get wrapped up with his old, youthful, treacherous scheming ways. A few tragedies helped accentuate the imbalance in his feelings. First, his most beloved wife, Rachel had died in her prime. Second, his first son Reuben had an incestuous relationship with his younger wife, Bilhah. Third, his uncouth only daughter Dinah had been date-raped by Prince Shechem, the Hivite, a heathen she had had defiantly dated![17] Fourth and finally, all of Jacob's wild sons – with the exception of Joseph and his younger brother Benjamin – had terribly avenged their sister's rape, murdering countless thousands in the country in a bloody massacre which had led to Jacob's voluntary exit unto Bethel, leaving Dinah behind! Joseph therefore, was the only trustworthy one in whom old Jacob had relished – and upon whom his soul and sole-companionship had depended.

In the developing countries where governmental care facility programs for the aged are far out of sight, adequate forecast and preparations ought to be made for the care and companionship of aged parents by their children. This responsibility should *not* be abandoned onto the only one caring child who is geographically resident within their vicinity. Such a child would no doubts soon become so burdened and encumbered with such enormous responsibilities that should be overseen by both they and their siblings.

Bless the young care-givers here in the United Kingdom. Bless you for the huge sacrifices you have made – and continue to make – towards the well-being of your parents, siblings – and loved ones. But again, I suggest that highlights of carers' plights and remunerations should be given more prominence in the national planning and budgets than currently are.

Similarly, ageing parents ought *not* deploy their proneness to loneliness as a tool of manipulation on *any* child. Naturally, God designed it that grown-up children owe it a strong sense of spiritual duty and moral responsibility to cater for their parents – *not* just in old age but at all times. As a child therefore, you should stop incurring upon your head, unpronounced parental curses due to your continued and deliberate neglect of the father and mother who gave you your *very* life. Take good care of your parents – whether young, middle-aged, ageing or aged. This is appropriate, well-directed honor!

Understandably, Jacob had exploited the youthfulness, willingness and singleness of *the* very responsible, kind-hearted Joseph to comply with his lack of appropriate companionship. Joseph had indirectly been victimized – even by the *very* father who had very much loved him.

10. *Victim of Mrs. Potiphar's sexual-attack allegation:*

If you'd been Joseph, wouldn't you have thought there had been a curse placed upon your life – particularly whenever you had been just about to settle down to doing what you're good at, something horrible had suddenly unsettled or uprooted you? There in Egypt, in his master's house, dedicatedly going about his assigned duties as a *'sold'* slave, Joseph had again become *the* victim of his boss' wife's intense sexual advances and threats!

What mind could have conceived of such dastardly act? Not Joseph's, in the very least! So righteous Joseph had turned down the over-sexed Mrs. Potiphar's requests to come and be defiled! *He'd continued to perform his daily routine with opened eyes!* Day after day still, her desire had intensified. God was looking. Angels were watching. The man of God was being passed through God's furnace without which he couldn't have been rightly moulded for his ultimate destiny! Joseph had persistently continued to refuse her suggestive advances, the Bible says. Then someday, when no one else had been in with them, Mrs. Potiphar could no longer continue to delay both the urge and the insults brought about by Joseph's continued resistance, she *had* made her deadly, calculated move:

> *"And it came to pass about this time, that Joseph went into the house to do his business; and there was none of the men of the house there within.*
>
> *And she caught him by his garment, saying, Lie with me: and he left his garment in her hand, and fled, and got him out …"*
>
> — GENESIS 39:11-12

In today's world, *sexting*, pestering, harassing and stalking another would have earned a restraining order – and possibly, some time in a psychiatric rehabilitation unit. Molesting and an eventual assault on a *'bond worker'* would have won Joseph a huge civil litigation. Character assassination put forward in a different libel suit should have been worth millions of pound sterling against Mrs. Potiphar. *CCTV* footages to corroborate her aggression – would have been turned in, accompanied by heavy compensation claims for defamation of character and emotional injuries. In a quick, unbelievable twist of events, the impudent-faced lady had turned the tide against the innocent slave. She had had him *'framed'* – and glazed! Joseph once again had become a victim of the crime of an evil conscience. His alleged crimes carried the heftiest penalty: the death sentence, in the Egypt of that day.

If you had been Joseph, what would have rummaged through your mind? Wouldn't you have queried: *'God, is this how You reward a faithful saint's perseverance to live a holy life?'*

Having listened to the rants of an unruly wife, Captain Potiphar had detained Joseph in jail until his execution papers would have been served. But first, he had *had* to sleep over the matter; the ultimate decision to snuff Joseph's life was entirely at his disposal! He had been both troubled and shaken, yet he had known something was amiss in the jigsaw puzzle involving *this* Joseph!

God had His eyes on His faithful steward. He again had intervened. Potiphar had not been able to sleep! The Joseph Potiphar had known had been faithful and disciplined. God had been with him. Everything under his influence had flourished.[18] *'Could there have been a mistake, somewhere?'* he'd reasoned. Still dazed, the Captain called the *Home Office* and asked that Joseph Jacob's *Residence of Abode Letter* be rescinded. He would serve time – and after this, be deported to Edom! Joseph had escaped the executor's blade somehow by the Hands that guided providence. He had been sent to Egypt's Maximum Security Prison, Cairo. Here, he would serve with the Pharaoh's top political detainees:

> *"And Joseph's master took him, and put him into the prison, a place where the king's prisoners were bound: and he was there in the prison."*
>
> — GENESIS 39:20

Once behind clamped metal doors, methinks Satan had thought it all finished – and had gone seeking for another victim whom he could torment. That had always been his thought pattern! But such crucial times are the times God reaches for His *'super charged turbo'* buttons: the invisible hands of the Creator of men's destinies had been busy carving out a niche for His most celebrated prisoner of all times. Potiphar had life-jailed Joseph and had thought it for a punitive demotion to the slave; God had planned His servant's jail-experience for a promotion. Potiphar had thought Joseph would become a *statistic*. God had meant Joseph to become a global *fact* to be reckoned with in the world of his days. Joseph had become a *political prisoner*, closest to his breakthrough – closest to the crest of Egypt's political seat of power. But God wasn't done with this gem of a man yet. He wouldn't spare him the tiniest tarnishing spot. He would still apply His refiner's fire! Joseph would yet fall another victim!

11. *Finally, Joseph had been a victim of broken trust by a potential helper:*

One powerful phrase you would find recurring all through the story of Joseph is:

"But the LORD was with Joseph ..."

— GENESIS 39:21

Whenever I have read this remarkable story and have come across that phrase, I have always loved to render it in two parts, thus: *"But the Lord"; "… with Joseph!"* The secret of his deliverance was that the Lord always showed up when all hopes had been but lost. Joseph had learned to always secure the presence of the LORD! God's steadfast faithfulness would yet open another door unto him if he would engage his innate gifting.

These past eleven years, Joseph's spiritual gift interpreting dreams had been very dormant since the urgency at hand required the use of his physical strength. Have you noticed that whenever strength from the flesh had been engaged, divine strength had been disengaged – and vice versa? But for his genuine, inquisitive and compassionate nature, Joseph's gift would be demanded for, even behind bars. You see, no devil could keep a keen, watchful, prayerful, godly man or woman down for so long: He or she is like a float! Floats must defy gravity and rise to the surface of the turbulence, no matter the intensity of the currents and the tosses of the waves! Joseph so genuinely cared for the well-being of other inmates that they had reposed their individual confidences in him! One day, he had been requested to interpret the dreams for a couple of officer-inmates who had wronged the Pharaoh: the offending Chief Butler and Chief Baker!

Joseph's interpretation had prophesied the butler's

restoration – and the baker's execution. It had only taken mere three days before those prophecies had come to pass!

Here's a lesson from this victimization Joseph had fallen prey to: It should be a counselor's delight to receive counselees voluntarily return to share with them testimonies of breakthroughs – and possibly, with a thanksgiving or appreciation *Prophetic seed offering*, appreciating God's grace upon such vessels! '*Counselees*' may also of their very accord render acts of benevolence to the vessels of God. This is Heaven's acceptable order. The counselor ought *not* present to counselees, *any* help requests, whatsoever! Neither should they make testifiers feel indebted to their recourse on the anointing they carry.

Joseph, under the crackling heat of the furnace had approached almost a breaking point. He had actually kissed God's protocol: *B-y-e!* He had pleaded with his 'counselee', the chief Butler:

> *"But think on me when it shall be well with thee, and shew kindness, I pray thee, unto me, and make mention of me unto Pharaoh, and bring me out of this house;*
>
> *For indeed I was stolen away out of the land of the Hebrews: and here also have I done nothing that they should put me into the dungeon."*
>
> — GENESIS 40:14-15

Joseph Achieves his Long-Awaited Destiny

God had never – and would never – share his glory with anyone! You would be heart-broken *if* you serve God and flesh, at the same time. A further two-year delay stint had been slammed upon Joseph while Heaven's angels had promptly wiped clean the Chief Butler's memory and offer of help unto him. The Bible says he'd forgotten all about Joseph. Whoa!

> *"Yet did not the chief butler remember Joseph, but forgat him."*
>
> — GENESIS 40:23

God alone – and no one else – would bring out and present His most-celebrated prisoner of all time out from that prison into the rich and wealthy palace. Who does that, but God? What length, width or depth would you reckon God unwilling to go, fill or occupy in order to have you well cut and shaped for your life's divine assignment? Are you prepared?

As I approach the end of this story, I remember the Son of God without blemish, sent ahead – and pleased of the Father to be bruised with many afflictions and victimizations like Joseph had, in order to prepare His Father God, a people!

Joseph's destiny had been fulfilled: *"He sent a man before them, even Joseph, who was sold for a servant: Whose feet they hurt with fetters: he was laid in iron: Until the time that his word came: the word of the Lord tried him"* (Psalms 105:17-19).

Man could have wronged Joseph. Negative circumstances could have blown him an ill-wind, but in all of these, he had chosen rather, to acknowledge the expedient hands of God alone initiating His divine counsel in him! In the fullness of time, he had been re-united with his father Jacob – and his kid brother, Benjamin. He had borne the burdens of his half-brothers and their families in his heart. He had *chosen* to forgive his offenders. He had calmed his brothers' agitated minds. He had pre-served a whole race. He had fulfilled his destiny. He had acted well *his* apportioned part in the preservation of the destiny of the nation of Israel, the Messiah, and even *you!*

Make your complete obedience to God count. You're not a misfit – or a mismatch!

**Portions of this chapter have been culled, excerpted, re-written and adapted to suit the purposes of this book from 'DESTROYING the Power of Delay: Possessing Your Canaan'. Copyright; granted.*

Chapter 7

Don't Trouble Your Posterity

*"If you want your children to turn out well, spend twice
as much time with them, and half as much money."*

— ABIGAEL VAN BUREN

Weaknesses in any parent could potentially be repeated in any of the children's lives if appropriate and adequate care is not taken! You have seen how that had panned out in Jacob's life. From conception, he had been a trickster. As he'd held onto his brother's heels in fetal position inside the amniotic bag they had both shared, no doubts exists in my sanctified mind that their mother had been sore troubled and restless throughout the gestation. Double-check your biblical accounts; you will find the confirmation of my assumption in *Genesis 25:20-26.* It was a double-dose-pill for Jacob – whose name's interpretation actually meant *trickster, liar, supplanter* and *cheat.* His grandfather too had been an impulsive, technical liar. So also had been his wife Rachel, the mother of Joseph and Benjamin who had been very emotionally manipulative and somewhat controlling of her husband once she'd discovered her womb had been shut while her sister, Leah's and her maids had kept on bearing children. So you see how easy it could have been for hereditary issues to trickle downward through the genes onto Joseph, too.

Have you noticed negative hereditary traits in you, very similar to your parents' or grannies'? If so, I challenge you this very hour to acknowledge those for what they are – and begin to appropriately address them in spiritual remedial actions! I have been able to show you in succinct details in the preceding chapter, how father Jacob's youthful and hereditary-traits left unaddressed, had caught up with him, over-spilling onto his posterity.

If you wouldn't trouble your posterity – that is a lineage of generations of your children, their children – and their children's children, here's a checklist of at least *FIVE* major behavioral patterns you *must avoid* like a plague:

1. ***Never retaliate their stupid acts at you with a word of curse or ill-saying:***

   What words of utterance had Jacob released upon his oldest son once he'd realized Ruben had had a carnal incestuous relationship with Bilhah, his younger step-mother? His ill-advised curse was recorded for our learning in *Genesis 49:3-4* thus:

"Reuben, you are my firstborn, my might, the beginning (the firstfruits) of my manly strength and vigor; [your birthright gave you] the preeminence in dignity and in power.

But unstable and boiling over like water, you shall not excel and have preeminence [of the firstborn], because you went to your father's bed; you defiled it — he went to my crouch!"

— GENESIS 49:3-4; AMPLIFIED VERSION

Read the last verse again with me: *"But unstable and boiling over like water, you shall not excel and have pre-eminence ..."*

What would you reckon the words of that pronouncement as — words of a blessing or a curse?

Doubtless, those were words of a curse. Parental curse, at that!

As I write to advise the parent(s), permit me to also take a moment to quip a word of counsel to the youngster(s). I know you for sure; you will sometimes misbehave — and misbehave very badly! But if you could quickly apologize to your parent(s), guardian(s) or any with legal parental responsibility over you when you realize you have been in the wrong, you would alleviate a lot of hot sticky mess blemishing your destiny for a very long haul.

If you have apologized and they have refused to accept or acknowledge your apology but have nevertheless proceeded to speak against you, then be rest assured; the Holy Bible re-assures:

"As the bird by wandering, as the swallow by flying, so the curse causeless shall not come."

— PROVERBS 26:2

Behavioral modification techniques that model acceptable behavior and speech patterns; calming and prevention techniques *via* consistent, fair and firm godly disciplinary training inculcate early in *any* child protective boundaries of love. When any parent(s) couple these with instilling within their children's little mind-frames from youth, the fear of the Lord, their parent-children relationship shall in the long run prove far richer than an outlandish word of hot wrath being heaved upon any child's spirit. To be very honest with you, speaking, dealing outlandish verbal, emotional or physical punches against your seed makes you a child abuser. That's how Heaven sees you! You are a victim, so undiscovered – a wreck, a step away from a locked jail cell! So also are the 'lovey-dovey' parents who refuse to administer a much-needed discipline appropriately, to their children or ward: you dwell in the doldrums of being marked as abusers of God's spiritual parental authority vested upon you! My heart breaks for you – so does God's!

If you do not personally know the Lord; allow proven, trusted, godly influences to surround your children. Journey with them to a living church where sound Sunday school is taught – and for their sakes, sit your bum down to enjoy (or endure) such services with them, disregarding your feelings! You will be wiser for your obedient actions in a decade's time, trust my words! Expose them to virtuous living. Wish them well from the depth of your heart. Never curse or speak a negative word over your children *when* they have done you wrong. Doing so is likened unto the proverbial black *mamba* which in attempts to fight off the attack a lone soldier ant, bites itself in the process – and dies of its own bite wounds.

Jacob's words of curse had an eternal repercussion on Rueben: he never regained his double-portion inheritance position as the firstborn. He had lost it to Joseph.

"Two wrong's never make a right," as the saying goes!

2. *Never choose 'favorite(s)' among your children:*

Never choose favorites – or preferences – among your children, grandchildren or great-grandchildren. This was Jacob's error as had been evidently portrayed to us in the Holy Scriptures. Picking favorite(s) amongst siblings ranks as #1 character weakness in parents and grand-parents. It wreaks havoc – and promotes rancor and an unhealthy rivalry in children.

You as a parent, *Nanna* or *Pappa* have got to fix *you* if you want it well, with your posterity!

A decade ago as I raised my five children single-handedly having suffered a bitter divorce, I laid them a sure foundation – and a firm rule of law. I made it unequivocally clear to both them and me: *"There ain't any favorites in this home: we're all equal before God – and daddy!"* It was very tough sometimes to reasonably manage the emotions of two sets of twin children – yes, you heard me quite rightly – who were aged 1+, 3 – and an older sister, barely 6. If you're perfect at math, that gives you an answer of an average age of five children as just under 3 years old.

This was the average occurrence any hour of any day, seven days of a blessed God-given week at ours: One child may have maliciously pinched the other on the arm – and had pretended it wasn't he or she who had committed the crime while the evidence had been as glaring as an owl could have been, to a bat! Another may not have tidied up after them – and had told an unscrupulous lie on a sibling, yet had pulled an innocent face with tears of denial streaking down their rotund cheeks! One of the boys in particular had enjoyed using the toilet and soiling the sides of the pristine white bowl. On some quicker occasions, he had loved sleepwalking – into the privacy room – and 'peeing' on the wooden laminate flooring heated by the under-board, floor-heating system.

How do you figure out fairness in all of these?

Well, sometimes, I must admit; it had been hard. It had been hard to separate my emotions from the bitterness of being single and all alone, encumbered with these lovely burdens of joy! It had also been hard separating the daily frustrations of just sheer tiredness from day-to-day routines supervised by the courts and her agents, for solid four years! Sometimes, I'd got it all wrong disciplining an innocent child I'd deemed as the offender while the real deal had walked off, leisurely. One tool had been sharper than my rationale, though – and I am glad I'd never at any point failed to gainfully employ its use. It was the Bible.

As I'd employed Biblical instructions – even if I had misjudged a child, my mistake had been swiftly corrected with a deserving apology. Many a time I'd bent my knees in front of the child I'd wronged, misjudged or wrongly punished – and had offered the words: *"I am sorry for wrongly punishing you when I should have punished ________."* I had cried a few times as I'd hugged the soft-hearted one, now in tears, sobbing!

Most other times though, I'd gotten the right offender to discipline. Equity and fairness had played out by reverentially following conjecture and a well-worn path of behavior, egged on by an inner witness. Most disciplinarian parents and grandparents would understand what I am talking about.

At such times, I had administered discipline with firmness and fairness.

With time however, both they and I had gotten better in the routine of understanding what the terms 'fairness', 'firmness', 'equity' and 'self-respect' entail. Today, with the older three already in their teenage-years and the last set of twins tottering on the brinks of becoming teenagers themselves, I am grateful to the Lord for firmness of discipline and the integrity to raise them, equal in the eyes of God, my unequivocal high expectation of – and love for them.

3. ***Never take sides with any of your children when they have disagreement(s):***

It means exactly what you read: never take sides in their disagreements! Now this does not at all equate your avoidance mediating reasonably and fairly in their squabbles. Some other times, you may just need to put your foot down, firmly, but lovingly. (I presume if the children have been well brought up by you, there never ever should have arisen *a* need for your foot to be rigidly put forward, stamped! A finger-tab on the issue should eternally resolve the natter, at least in my household!)

4. ***Don't die intestate: write and update your will if you need to:***

From time to time, people die intestate bequeath-ing a lot of squabbles and grief to their children with regards to who gets what in their inheritance or estate. Don't cause your postcrity un-necessary pain and trouble that would fester for generations to come. Write a will.

Write your will held securely by your solicitor, attorney or lawyer. The bequeathal of lands, estate, company shares and inheritance must be written in black and white, in a will, held securely, by your attorney. For a token fee, most solicitors would be more than willing to help you avoid "the curse of inheritance" alighting upon your children – and pos-terity. You don't have to be rich to afford writing a will. Most banks with which you hold a current account – for example, the Barclays Bank in England offers – "Will Writing" services freely, as part of cer-tain premium accounts that are available to account holders. Quite worth finding out from the Customer Services desk of your bank.

Remember again, if you have just a nice shoestring and a couple of shiny, leather ties, you need to write a will on who gets what after you're gone!

5. *Never forget to intercede for your posterity, daily:*

These days of *your* tottering at the borders of senior citizenry and graceful ageing, you seem to have more hours of the day than when you were at youth, don't you? If you do – and you should; why don't you endeavor to take a portion of time, as you please each day, to pray and intercede for your posterity?

Pray for your children, grand-children – and great grandchildren. Pray also for their parents: your sons and daughters – including in-laws. Write their names out on a piece of paper – or in your diary. Carry that diary on you as you sit on the front porch or in your garden or yard interceding for them, name by name, city by city – and by workplaces. Sometimes, God will give you a word or a scripture for them. It is not wrong to dial them up at that time – whatever times of the day it is the Lord has placed their memory in your heart. Tell them what message the Lord has given you for them. I am sure they would be glad to know that Grannie always bears them up in prayers.

Ensure that you bind your posterity together firmly as a bunch, with the cords of prayer.

Chapter 8

Disproportionate
Friendships

"The prospects of a godly friendship are exponential in size, length, width, depth and height!"

— Sammy O. Joseph

We possess our physical senses for a reason: to adequately function in a physical world. We dare not wish them away: they're a part of our Creator's endowment-package unto our humanity. Feelings essentially accompany the stirring of our physical senses: the feelings created by *smell, touch, sight, hearing* or the emotions stirred within us by a great speech, song, word, and a piece of literature – not forgetting the overwhelming feelings created by a familiar fragrance!

Similarly, our emotional and sexual beings would be incomplete without the important part our feelings play. Thus, we have strong feelings of love, acceptance, well-being and fulfilment in our emotional beings. We may also have feelings of fear and premonition – or even feelings of danger and anger!

You cannot afford to so soon dismiss the importance of the interplay of your feelings in choosing affiliations and meaningful covenant relationships. The friendship or associations you keep will either enhance your destiny – or mar it altogether. Those words sound harsh, but no other seems truer!

Carefully and prayerfully choose your friends. By the term *friends*, I am not talking of *Facebook, Twitter, Pinterest, Google*+ social-media friends. Most of those on there are simply acquaintances; you may not find them when your chips are down. Some of them do not even know your middle name! But when I use the term *'friend'*, I mean those whom the Lord by His special grace has allowed you to play a cognizable part in their lives as they have in yours. I talk about individuals whose souls are con-joined with yours as you together travel this journey called life! Rabbi Jesus' admonition: *"Be ye therefore wise as a serpents, and harmless as a doves"* cannot be ruled out, in ensuring you do *not* join your destiny with disproportionate, unevenly-weighted people in friendships! [1]

The inherent fault with most disproportionate, unevenly-weighted, unequally-yoked friendships is the ambiguity therein that while these friends are not essentially evil in orientation; yet, the final destination or port of call you would be arriving at would definitely *not* be the same as you had conceived when you had set out! More importantly, the time, effort and costs of re-routing towards your original destination should definitely leave you out of pocket, emotion and strength. The betrayal of commitment and trust midway in marriages alone accounts for one of the reasons there be so many emotionally wounded hearts, throbbing heads and insane minds in our world! But you don't have to add to a deplorable statistic. That's the main reason I have asked you to "Go slow" on the friendships and relationships you *find*, *assign*, *keep* and *maintain*.

Some of the very few questions I would love you to calmly ask yourself before adventuring out with a friendship proposition include:

- *Are we both setting our faces and minds up towards the same destination?*

- *Am I interested in their pursuits as they are in mine?*

- *Do I see myself committing unto — and supporting them in making sure they realize their goals and aspirations? — and, finally;*

- *What is my gain in this friendship?*

Let us briefly examine them, each.

1. *Sameness of Goals*

Heading the same direction with those you desire to befriend is a great asset – and a most vital tool. The Bible tells the story of Jonah – a prophet sent of God to Nineveh to go warn the prominent city of an impending judgment from God in form of total destruction and annihilation. But the stubborn prophet had some other willful ideas: he wouldn't go to Nineveh. He'd found a merchant vessel that was destined for Tarshish (that is current day Spain). Notice, he was a runaway prophet on a journey – and on a relation-ship! Whether or not Prophet Jonah had hibernated on that ship or struck new friendships wasn't the deal; as long as he had stepped aboard that ship, both theirs and his destiny had now become intricately and dangerously intertwined. Needless to say, that ship had been troubled in high waters solely for the reason of Jonah being on board! Same it is between you and whoever you choose to find, assign, keep and maintain friendship or relationship with.[2]

Now, here's a pertinent question: "What would you reckon those merchants were *en route* Tarshish for?"

I believe you'd say for business; that is to sell, make gains – and better their lot! And you've perfectly rightly said!

Now here's the bottom-line of the teaching I am getting your mind to conceive: by the time Jonah had been discovered on the lowest deck of the ship, the damage had been done. Their vessel's cargos had in no time being consigned to poignant memories. Each merchant had suffered huge material losses; they had barely escaped by the reason of their teeth! Even the ship's insurance firm had not a light bill to settle! Everyone had been grossly decimated for the sake of a naughty, selfish man who had been at direct, head-on, loggerheads with the God of Heaven.

The bottom-line of Jonah's story? Beware of absconders and 'run-aways' should they endeavor to gain entrance aboard your ship!

2. *Sameness of Pursuits*

Are they interested in my pursuits as I am in theirs?

There are certain people who are essentially called "helpers" or "encouragers". They achieve their best niche being supportive pillars that bear the load, "shoulders upon which the burden rests." In a ministry setting, they are the dependable financial partners. For a prophet in training just aspiring to emerge from the pit, they would be 'connectors', forging unalloyed alliances between the pit and the palace. They always have a strong, heaven-sent word to say on your behalf.

They may also be sent of the Lord to bring you an unpleasant word of rebuke or correction in righteousness – even though they may hesitate to fulfil this sometimes essential ministry! Beware to not disrespect their 'ministry of help', generally!

To an unsaved soul, it is someone like me and you, sent with a word of witness for their deliverance and salvation!

If you're in unbelief like General Joshua of old, feel free to demand off them an answer to the tune: *"Are you for us or against us?"* Scripture recorded the conversation between General Joshua and the Angel of the Lord:

> *"And it came to pass, when Joshua was by Jericho, that he lifted up his eyes and looked, and behold, there stood a man over against him with his sword drawn in his hand: and Joshua went unto him and said unto him, Art thou for us, or for our adversaries?*
>
> *And he said, Nay; but as captain of the hosts of the LORD am I now come. And Joshua fell on his face to the earth and did worship, and said unto him, what saith my lord unto his servant?*
>
> *And the captain of the LORD's host said unto Joshua, Loose thy shoe from off thy foot: for the place whereon thou standest is holy. And Joshua did so."*
>
> — JOSHUA 5:13-14

Do *not* irritate these mercenaries of help. Some of you who are so verbose would need to really hold the muscle of your tongue really tightly well shut, behind the doors of your dentition so as not to put them off by your much talking. They are mission-active, not talkative. Do *not* attempt to abuse them by attempting to take undue advantage of their availability. Do *not* covet after generosity placed at your disposal.

Any country of the world that I had traveled to and had been picked up by either my friends or host ministers, I'd always made it a point of priority to *not* request an added favor that would digress them out of their planned routes. It is called considerateness. Be considerate and not covetous.

Accept with gratitude the undeserved help these special agents of Heaven offer you without *any* reservations. These helpers of destiny normally would never request for reciprocity nor would they play the common 'offer-for-reward game'. Such was the friendship of youthful David with Jonathan, the son of King Saul – without whose help, he'd never had become Israel's king.

Despite the fact that they demand no repayment, you would do well to reciprocate – and be appreciative of – their kindness. Do not take them for granted.

Many years after the demise of Jonathan, King David had shown gratitude and magnanimity towards Jonathan's lame son, Mephibosheth. He had requested him and his family to sit at his dining table all the days of their lives! That translated among other benefits: free meals, no tax and their mortgage debts paid off in full! Hectares of landed portions were also being negotiated by the king's consort to be returned for their heritage! This is what bible scholars refer to as covenant friendship.[3]

Are you that kind of a friend – a covenant friend to your friends?

Little wonder God had established David's kingdom forever unto Christ's! For the records, that Kingdom has no end in sight. That's as best as I can define the impact a covenant friendship could produce. It is exponential in both increment and size. It outlives a thousand generations of parties involved.

Again, are you a covenant partner to a friend, I dare ask?

I have always not forgotten to mention that I will stand at the Judgment Seat of Christ ready to share portions of my soul-winning and soul-establishment gains with as many of my faithful covenant part-ners as have enabled me spread this Gospel of the Kingdom by way of their unflinching support, on that glorious day. The very truth is that not only will they benefit, but their posterity too, to a thousand generations!

This is a "*sure word*" which cannot be broken![4]

3. *Sameness of Commitment*

Are they committed unto supporting me and ensuring I

realize my life's goals and aspirations as I am committed unto theirs?

You will be in a pitiable frame of mind to decline a potential, fruitful alliance because of petty, minor, non-essential differences. There are bound to be differences of characters and tastes between any new persons or people just meeting, anyway! When you want to factor in 'interests' into your significant choices of lasting covenant friendships, zero in on the interplay of sameness of *'essentials'*. Notice the emphasis on my choice of the word 'essentials'; in other words, you may differ in your non-essential desires, wants and preferences; that's pretty smooth as long as your focus on sameness of commitment to the essential factors and goals cuts perfect!

Additionally, foundational essential pursuits too should be mutual; not forced, coerced or demanded! It even gets better if you – or they – are willing to learn from, adapt to and incorporate each other's interests, hitherto foreign to both parties. Say for example, they are *kinetic-impulsive* – that is to say, out-doorsy and active riding a horse or a Harley Davidson at a local Bikers' club while you are *esthetically-impressed* – that is, appreciating the finer world of the works of arts, nature, music and literature; there's no harm role-learning, role-sharing and role-swap-ping each other's preferred activities; provided doing so originated from genuine hearts of mutual appreciation of each other's interests! Actually, one

of the healthy signs to all profitable, covenant relationships – those mutual trusts – which we all aspire
unto, is that they elucidate undoubted commitment
and compassion, in enormous proportions!

4. *Surety of Reward*

What is my gain in this friendship?

If all there exists on your drawing boards are *their*
gains – and nothing in the stakes for you, that's a
sure sign of a disproportionate alliance you're about
signing for!

The reason your friendship fails to yield returns may
be because you are too docile to request what's right-
fully yours in an alliance or a joint partnership into
which you're expected to reputably invest. Even Jesus'
disciples had taken Him to task on this very issue.
They had inquired of their Master: *"What's our gain
if we forsook all – and followed you?"* Sure enough, they
had gotten a reply off the immortal lips of the Savior:

> *"Yes, Jesus said to them, and I tell you that
> anyone who leaves homes or brothers or sisters
> or mother or father or children or fields for me
> and for the gospel will receive much more in this
> present age.*
>
> *He will receive a hundred times more houses,
> brothers, sisters, mothers, children and fields – and
> persecutions as well; and in the age to come he
> will receive eternal life"*

> — Mark 10:29-30; GNB

Chapter 9

Radical Responses to Challenging Times

"You have to decide what your highest priorities are and have the courage — pleasantly, smilingly, non-apologetically, to say "no" to other things. And the way you do that is by having a bigger 'yes' burning inside."

— Dr. Stephen R. Covey

Were I to ask: *"What part of this book has impacted you the most?"*; would you be able to say, without a second thought or a blink?

Well, it should be obvious that I do tremendously feel tugged onboard the vessel of the 'ministry of helps' – probably not essentially in the way you've always thought or conceived of it. No minister of God could so function efficiently well, dissing away the 'ministry of helps' – the ministry of compassion. The core of my passion for my readership, listening and ministry audiences centers upon my thirst to ensure that each of these groups actualizes their God-given destiny. This I endeavor to do through offering guidance and helpful counseling pieces of advice *via* the ingenious life experiences I have been privileged to gather over a quarter of a century now, since I have been in the Gospel ministry. I have in earlier chapters and paragraphs counseled you with what I deemed to be lesson-teaching, life-changing, true stories including:

- Nina who had endured years of brutal abuse from her very own father at such a tender age whom she had forgiven – and had even led to Christ towards the very end of his life;

- My friend, late Pastor Phillip's unexpected passing;

- The male and female genders' surrealistic expectations at the onslaught of mid-life crises, corroborating my thoughts with due reference to the work of the editor at *Body & Soul* magazine, Australia. I also referred to the 'midlife' crises experienced by the shepherd-boy David *vis-à-vis* the embattled couple Nabal and Abigail of biblical times;

- Not shrinking back the truth on how to approach and solve the problems involving contending, disgruntled family members. I had cited the debilitating, large scale-ripple effects such a dysfunctional family as Joseph's could feel in sharpening destinies of all involved;

- Examining in concise details the emotional confusions encasing separation and divorce of married couples – and lastly,

- Wisdom bordering on making, choosing and keeping friends in *Disproportional Friendships.*

In this closing chapter, I am going to attempt inter-weaving every preceding page; all encompassed into the next few lines. And as you may surmise, it is going to be a short summary of the entire book in useful, practicable pieces of advice, tried and tested over time!

My suggestions for radical responses to challenging times include:

1. ***Not disowning your errant teenager child undergoing a turbulence:***

    I am yet to find a pilot who bailed out of his cockpit abandoning his airplane experiencing an air-turbulence. But I have met a few parents who have copped out of parenting their teenaged child undergoing hormonal release-spurts in their blood veins. (Isn't that the summary of what 'adolescence' entails? Weren't you once an adolescent, yourself?)

    Somehow as parents, we have come to find it easier

to love the obedient child. On the other hand, we easily get run-down in our emotions towards one, disobedient. If you've done a thorough job of raising your children from very tender ages, you would need practically nothing to worry your mind about one of them turning errant when they have grown older and left the shades of your tutelage for College or University. The infallible training manual firmly instructs you the parent(s) to: *"Train up a child in the way he should go, when he is old, he will not depart from it."*[1] In other words, God's Spirit has a way of re-routing errant children or wards onto the pathway of righteousness, in due time. It's not in your power to do; it's in His almighty, unfailing power to effect that turnaround in them!

In the interim, how should you – as a parent – respond to a disobedient teen-aged or adult child, then?

If you neglected, disowned or forsook your child when their teenage hormones raged, you would have caused them, almost, an irreparable emotional damage by the time their senses had returned to them, in latter years! Quit thinking parenting is a job signed for until your child turns 18. Nothing is as farther from the truth than that. Godly parenting while letting go of the emerging young adult does *not* end "at 18"– but "until you die." True parents do *not* stop caring – and praying – for a child undergoing 'turbulence', despite the heartbreak they've caused – or may further cause!

Same goes for spiritual parenting! Spiritual parents exercising spiritual jurisdiction over an errant son or daughter in the faith do not cease praying and interceding for them despite their saying or doing the detestable! Prophet Samuel had not ceased to pray for his errant, disobedient, spiritual children who had rejected him and his sons as judges in the land until the day he had drawn his very last breath. The aggrieved, heart-broken prophet had said doing otherwise is tantamount to sinning *"against the LORD"* (1 Samuel 12:23).

Pray for your cozy – as well as crazy biological and / or spiritual children! Do *not* utter a word of disfavor on their lives though they probably deserved it! Wait for their 'heart-change' patiently. With you loving them with the *agape* love of God, you will find them revert to your doorstep after many days, months or even years! You *must* remain steadfast in love and forgiveness; these are a significant part of the huge price *true* parents pay!

2. ***Not evil entreating those who have maligned you:***

God orchestrates people into our lives by His divine will for a reason, season, session – or a lifetime. You must be spiritually aware for what reason(s) God had brought *any* into your life. Relationships go through many seasons – including loving, hurts and offences; but also forgiveness, healing and restoration.

If you have been abused, maligned or broken; intercede for those who have violated, stolen from or 'murdered' a part of you. Pray that they be released from the strongholds that have had a firm grip upon them.

And in honor of the call of God upon my life, may I further request you to choose to forgive them – even if they wouldn't apologize for the wrong done you. The basic reason is obvious: there has never been any easier route to detour into soul rancor and pain other than through the bypass of unforgiveness. Unforgiveness thrives on the roots of bitterness, resentment and hurts. These roots are toxic. Medical sciences have been able to show links between cure-defying internal organ ailments and beguiled, bitter-spirited, gall-blighted folk. Diametrical findings are revealed also of patients' quick recovery when they are of joyous and a light spirit!

Don't send yourself to an early grave. Forgive! Forgive – and forget!! As you recreate the body through exercise, you can train your mind through conscious, re-creative, selective delete! The lesser you think, ponder and replay such horror incidents in your mind, the healthier you will become. The poor may malign the rich – and vice versa. The races may through hatred press hard at one another's jugular veins. The employer may defraud the employee – or indeed the king, the subject, as in Uriah's case. Possessing the spirit of understanding to *forgive* and *forget offences* – like I am sharing with you – will set you up on high; higher than your maligner, abuser or defrauder!

Young David would not execute *'his master'* King Saul in revenge, even though the opportunity twice availed itself to him. Instead, the anointed of God demonstrated his unshakeable innate understanding that God's long hands of vengeance will someday wrap itself in a tight grip around Saul's neck. He had verbalized his convictions thus:

> *"David said furthermore, As the LORD liveth, the LORD shall smite him; or his day shall come to die; or he shall descend into battle and perish.*
>
> *The LORD forbid that I should stretch forth mine hand against the LORD's anointed ..."*
>
> — 1 SAMUEL 26:10-11

How could anyone have accurately foretold the actual war-incident that would eventually involve Saul and ultimately lead to his death except he had possessed the spirit of understanding? Likewise, I've ratified my calling unto you, warning you of the dire strait wherein you dwell if you do not forgive your maligner – and forget the hurt. Your duty it is to find an acceptable way of aggressively pursuing peace with everyone, *"looking diligently lest any man fail of the grace of God: lest any root of bitterness springing up trouble you and thereby many be defiled"* (Hebrews 12:15).

3. ***Not ignorant of knowing when to act – and acting appropriately:***

Imagine you were a resident of Carmel town of old. You'd woken up one crisp, spring morning to compare newspaper-headlines about a bloodbath that had painted your hitherto quiet village, red overnight. Almost all the newspapers' summary-headlines had read:

> ***"Innocent Heads Rolled at Nabal Shearing & Dairy Farms Alongside Wicked Boss', In an Onslaught Caused by a Hungry Fugitive General!"***

You'd wondered when your peaceful neighborhoods had suddenly become a battleground.

But no, you needn't worry. One wise lady who possessed an astute mind and a spirit of understanding had saved a potential bloodbath with a deft, wise move. Abigail would *not* sit back idly and watch evil befall Carmel's residents, Nabal and the vast staffers that have made their family enterprise grow so vast. What a *savior* she had been!

Abigail had swiftly intervened. She'd swooped into positive action before an upset, hungry and angry mercenary-fugitive warrior could press the destructive button in order to save the life of her wicked husband Nabal. She had done this *not* because Nabal had loved her; but rather, because she had possessed an understanding of the mechanics of covenant relationships.

Let's dissect her wise moves in the spirit of under-standing:

First, she had honored David by lighting off her ass with haste – and had made obeisance to him with her face to the ground *(1 Samuel 25:23).* She must have indeed been a very humble woman.

Second, she had owned her husband's foolishness as hers – and had then "prayed" David to forgive her trespass *(1 Samuel 25:28a).*

Here's a question that would conflict your modern-day mind: *Do you think she was actually to blame for Nabal's well-intended stupidity insulting and disgracing David's men as he had done to them shaving them and stripping them?*

In all honesty, no. But an understanding heart knows better.

When Prophet Daniel had offered his intercessory prayer to God, he had confessed the iniquities of his forefathers, as his – and his current generation's *(Daniel 9:1-17).*

Third, she had declared her innocence that she'd not personally met any of David's ten-man emissary earlier sent to Nabal to request for his assistance. She'd then quickly hinted David of the summary state-of-affair of her marriage to Nabal the "fool" *(1 Samuel 25:25).*

And would you think anything wrong with her disclosure?

I hope not!

Fourth, she had appeased the anger of David acknowledging his strengths with pin-pointed, precise, prophetic insight *(1 Samuel 25:26 & 28).*

Fifth, she had presented David with essential, life-preserving gift items: food for hungry stomachs. Her gift of a food-bank had been more than lavish: 200 loaves, 2 bottles of wine, 5 sheep ready dressed, 5 measures of parched corn, 100 clusters of raisins and 200 cakes of figs *(1 Samuel 15:18).*

Notice the relevance of the giver's gift to the receiver's need! She had given a huge food supply to a huge, hungry rebel-force. No wonder God had preserved her!

Abi had proven she hadn't been a misfit to Nabal, after all! Need you any more cues?

4. ***Not being ignorant of knowing when to speak – and speaking rightly:***

An astute woman filled with the spirit of understanding, Abigail had kept the details of her *"Rescue Mission"* a top secret, away from Nabal's knowledge because she had a perfect control over the reins of her heart! She hadn't dared divulge unto Nabal until she had returned from the mediation trip, when he had been sober from his heavy intoxication!

You may have ruined great, God-given salvation plans by being too mouthy! Learn from Abigail.

Her timing to inform Nabal of incidents couldn't have been more perfect! By the spirit of understanding, Abigail had realized that *any* who maligns, restrains, pursues or harms the anointed of the Lord, should have their souls slung out *"as out of the middle of a sling."*[2] According to the *word of knowledge* that had been spoken by Abigail, the "Righteous Judge" had deemed fit that the *'angel of death'* should snuff life out of Nabal on, exactly, the tenth day of his cursing and railing on those ten fainting soldiers sent by David![3]

And after she had delivered her emotional farewell speech to the guerilla leader of the wilderness, dear Abigail had not minced words with the depth of her affection for David. She had requested the future-king:

> *"… but when the LORD shall have dealt well with my lord, then remember thine handmaid"*
>
> — I SAMUEL 25:31

5. ***Not being blindfolded when carefully choosing your friends:***

When you're considering choosing friends, please ensure you have carefully taken into consideration such factors that would categorically endear you to everyone as *not* a misfit. Ponder carefully upon: *Sameness of Goals, Sameness of Pursuits, Sameness of Commitment and Surety of Reward!*

Chapter 10

Steepy, You Are
Not a Mismatch

"But God, Who is rich in mercy, for his great love wherewith he loved us."

— Apostle Paul; Ephesians 2:4

My message to you even now in this closing chapter remains: *"You are not a mismatch – neither are you a misfit!"* I am as adamant and rock-solid about my declaration upon you as a rockgoat on the surface of a steep!

Your behavior may have been summed up as *"erratically steepy"* – maybe that's even your nickname, it wouldn't make a difference. You love living life at the very edge – possibly on many fronts. You like pushing boundaries – with the aim of goring through like the bullfighting four-legged in the yearly *Carnaval del Toro,* in Spain. It doesn't matter what your sex is; you're wild, disregarding and rotten. You know it's true. Even in your quieter reflective moments, you don't seem to understand how you've traversed your way unto transforming into this monster welling up daily on the inside of you, consuming you. You just don't seem to 'get it' why folk are always on your case.

My friend, is that you?

I have some piece of *Goodnews* for you: No matter where you are, what you have done or left undone; no matter your race, nationality or ethnicity, no matter what label people have affixed and stuck on you, you are *not* a mismatch – neither are you a misfit!

I have intimated you throughout the pages of this book, real-life stories of different individuals even *you* would have labeled as *misfits!* But thank God, they didn't have to answer to such a tag because it actually is what it is: just an ordinary name-tag!

I read of the story of a very ravishing, beautiful, rich lady the other day. She had sourced her easy money from servicing men at the very top. She knew her clientele – and they knew her for who she was. She answered any name her different rich dates chose to call her for a time, only. She could afford travels, holidays and dinner-nights. But her heart was lonely, hurt and broken. The happy face was just a façade.

She had longed for – and had wanted something much more real and serene. She'd not been totally alone though; within her were fully resident seven, tough alien beings. She answered to her christian baptismal name: Mary, but that hadn't been enough to hold the fort against the wicked demons that had tormented her. If I am right, I understand she had suffered the influences of confused multiple personalities. She couldn't have ever been allowed to be her true self at any given time.

She had dreamt of the day of her complete, total recovery. In fact, she had downed meds attempting to soothe her aches – but she had only felt more trapped in her mind. That had been the summary of her life until she had met one Man that had revamped her entire life! The Savior, Jesus Christ, had through His supernatural power cleansed and restored her mind to total newness. Alas, there was an aura of total peace and joy!

Mary Magdalene had been healed from seven tough demons that had always been responsible for her proud attitude, lying tongue and hands that were quick to grab another woman's man in an adulterous sexual escapade. Her heart had been devious and filled with mischievous wicked imaginations; feet, swift to do mischief: false witnessing, testifying and striking discordant chords within closest family circles and friendships.[1]

Just one encounter with Jesus – and all aliens had abandoned garrison. You see, the Bible says our bodies belong to God – and as such asks us to *"glorify God in your body, and in your spirit, which are God's."*[2] But we haven't got the power to do that! We needed the power in the cleansing Blood of the Lamb that was shed for the taking away of our sins before our bodies and spirit can attain that state wherein they would glorify God!

"You are not a mismatch – neither are you a misfit!" I have been sent to proclaim to you at this hour! And you're neither alone! God's Holy Spirit through Jesus Christ will drive away all your abnormalities, disorders, sicknesses, afflictions and pain; if you allow Him.

Mary Magdalene *had* allowed Jesus into her heart. Her life had not remained the same again. Old things had passed away, all things had become new![3] At the same instance, Her spiritual eyes had been opened; she could *see* her very own nakedness had been clothed. There had been no more need for incomprehensible proud attitude and looks. Her tongue had been set free from guile. She had become holy in her desires – now she only desired to sit at the feet of Jesus Christ and learn from Him, the Words of life.

"To whom little is forgiven, the same loveth little."

— LUKE 7:47

And converse should be true: *"To whom much is forgiven, the same loves much!"*

My prayer to God for you this day is that you will recognize indeed, your truest incomparable worth; that you're neither a misfit – nor a mismatch in the Kingdom of our loving Father. You're an unquantifiable gem: yes, that's who you are! And if you would love to ask the LORD Jesus Christ into your heart, bow down your head right away – and pray aloud this simple prayer with me, wherever you may be:

"Dear Lord Jesus,

I am at my wits' end. I hereby do open the door of my heart unto You, now; please come in. Forgive me my sins. Cleanse – and save me! Write my name in the Book of Life. Thank you so very much!

Amen!"

If you prayed that prayer from your heart by faith, you've become a saved child of God. Write me today to: *'reverendsammy@harvestways.org'*

I simply can't wait to read from you.

Congratulations!

References

Chapter 1

—

Chapter 2

[1] Isaiah 46:9-10

Chapter 3

[1] Genesis 50:10

[2] 1 Samuel 25:1

[3] 2 Kings 2:23-24

[4] 2 Kings 2:25

[5] Matthew 14:13

[6] Amos 3:4-7

[7] Job 2:13

[8] Shakespeare's Twelfth Night, 1602; Act 1, scene 1, 1–3 Duke Orsino

Chapter 4

[1] Deuteronomy 23:2-4

[2] http://www.bodyandsoul.com.au/sex+relationships/wellbeing/female+midlife+crisis,7441 accessed Thursday November 6, 2014 @ 14.00hrs GMT

Chapter 5

[1] Joshua 14:14 & 15:54-55

[2] The correct answer is the last bullet point option.

[3] 1 Samuel 25:3; Amplified Version.

[4] 1 Samuel 25:3

[5] 1 Peter 3:4

[6] 1 Samuel 25:3

7. *1 Samuel 17:25*
8. *1 Samuel 18:14*
9. *1 Samuel 18:28-29*
10. *2 Samuel 6:20-23*
11. *Proverbs 11:14*

Chapter 6

1. *Exodus 3:6*
2. *Acts 9:16*
3. *Genesis 37:3*
4. *Genesis 37:4*
5. *1 Samuel 10:14-16*
6. *Genesis 37:11*
7. *Luke 2:51*
8. *Genesis 37:25*
9. *Amos 6:1-7*
10. *1 Samuel 13: 4-14*
11. *Numbers 3:4*
12. *Hebrews 12:29*
13. *Joel 3:3*
14. *Genesis 25:29-34*
15. *Matthew 26:14-16*
16. *Jeremiah 30:7*
17. *Genesis 34:1-end*
18. *Genesis 39:2-5*

Chapter 7

—

Chapter 8

1. *Matthew 10:16*
2. *Read the entire book of Prophet Jonah*
3. *2 Samuel 9:1-13*
4. *2 Peter 1:19*

Chapter 9

[1] *Proverbs 22:6*

[2] *1 Samuel 25:29*

[3] *1 Samuel 25:38*

Chapter 10

[1] *Proverbs 6:16-19*

[2] *1 Corinthians 6:20*

[3] *2 Corinthians 5:17*

Worship with Us if You're in our City

**The Harvestways Int'l Church
(Birmingham, U.K.)**
Holloway Hall
Northfield, Birmingham,
England, United Kingdom
B31 1TT
Sundays: 12 noon
Home Cell Friday Prayer Meeting: 7pm
Tel: (+44) 7758195466 / 7854675159
e-mail: admin@harvestways.org

**The Harvestways Int'l Church
(Nigeria)**
1 Harvest Way, Off Elewura Street
Behind Zartech / GLO Office,
Off Elewura Street
Challenge, Ibadan, Oyo State,
Nigeria, West Africa.
Sundays: 9am
Tuesdays: 6pm
e-mail: nigeria@harvestways.org

Other Books by the Author

Other books by the author are available at any Christian bookshop near you, *Pulse Publishing House* locations or from our website: *harvestways.org*

When the Chips Are DOWN

Based upon Jeremiah's observations in his elegiac poetic book of Lamentation, the author attempts to both depict the descriptions and manifested-traits of one whose chips are down! *We may do well to arm our minds with a re-assurance of the possibility of experiencing at least a molting experience – just like the bald eagle – in our lifetime. Our individual reactions however, to adversity – and what we do with such rich experiences – are of great consequences that will impact the life we currently live and that futuristic life eternal!"* You will be enraptured by the way the author has deployed sheer literary genus and a sharp, enrapturing writing style to describe the intuitive bald eagle – how he triumphs over his gruesome molting season in the wild. Learn in this book, your very personalized "way of escape" provided by the loving Heavenly Father out of the feelings of despair, despondency, desolation and depression.

(110 pages)

APPRECIABLE Gifts

Seekers in quest of attaining inner peace with the heavenly Father, deepening satisfaction in their friendships/relationships, healings from life's brokenness – enhancing their sexuality and marriages need search no further. Within the pages of *Appreciable Gifts* lie your missing trophies!

Irrespective of your status in life, if your heart desires to learn the most essential tips on how to 'spruce up' your 3-D relationships: vertical, horizontal and downwards, *'Appreciable Gifts'* will show you how! Read about: *The Greatest Gift of All, The Gift of Restoration, The Gift of a True Friendship, The Gift of Sex & Sexuality in Committed Relationships, and; Cultivating the Gifts of Thanksgiving & Gratitude.*

Read and apply guideposts on the parameters of offering, accepting, cherishing, maintaining – and abounding in gifts! The messages therein will positively impact your relationships for a lifetime!

(183 pages)

DESTROYING the Power of DELAY

This book is an expository piece of work, written in a scriptural, thought-provoking style. The author aimed at sharing with you from more than fifteen years of counseling in ministry, how to avoid the endearing long arms of delay; and if you're already entangled in a wild romance with the hated alien, the quickest way of escape from him.

Furthermore, real–life issues such as *'Causes of Delay'*, *'Who Should Care for the Elderly?'*, *'Wisdom Handling Inextricable Covenant Relationships'*, *'Liberating Financial Management and Dealing with Indebtedness'* are adequately discussed. Others topics include: *'How to Effectively Handle Mid-life Crisis, Depression, Barrenness'* - et cetera!

(220 pages)

GIDEON: Releasing the Potentials Within You

This book draws analogies from the life of Gideon (one of Israel's Judges) and applies them to how you can effectively release the hidden potentials within you. Written in easy, straightforward, simple language, you will find basic practical insights that will help lift you above common mediocrity levels in life!

(176 pages)

Before You Step into Someone Eles's Shoes

This book contains *easy-to-do* guides on how you will not repeat the costly mistakes made by others faced with a fresh opportunity to begin anew after suffering a heavy setback. We have also provided essential checklists to anyone willing to *step into shoes* ordained of God for them – as well as checkmating the mutineers!

(46 pages)

Download PULSE On-line, freely at www.harvestways.org

Become a *Sammy Joseph Ministries* Vision Partner

Our commitment is to:

- Pray – and cover you daily in prayers, that God's undeniable blessings be upon your you and your household.

- Keep ministering the Word of God diligently.

- Minister to you once a month via a telephone call from us.

- Minister to you in a personal newsletter from Dr. Sammy Joseph – at least quarterly.

- Issue you an official partner certificate.

- Offer you from time to time, special, discounted gifts for your spiritual growth and upliftment through our website, programs and outreaches.

Your commitment is to:

- Pray for us always.

- Be committed to support our broadcasts, meetings and outreaches in your area.

- Support us financially with your monthly 'seed' as said in Philippians 4:17.

- Always speak positive words of affirmation on the ministry, Dr. Joseph – and his family.

If you would love:

- To join or help us plant a branch of The Harvestways Int'l Church in your region;

- Become a vision partner / supporter of Sammy Joseph Ministries; or

- Become a volunteer at any of our outreaches.

Please write:

Sammy Joseph Ministries
P.O. Box 15129
Birmingham
West Midlands, England
B45 5DJ
admin@harvestways.org
Call: (+44) 7758195466 / 7854675159

THANK YOU!

Contact Addresses

PULSE Publishing House

In the United Kingdom

Pulse Publishing House
Sammy Joseph Ministries
Box 15129
Birmingham, England
U.K
B45 5DJ
Tel: (+44) 7758195466 / 7854675159
pulsepublishinghouse@ harvestways.org

In Nigeria

Pulse Publishing House
1 Harvest Way,
Off Elewura Street
Behind Zartech / GLO Office,
Challenge, Ibadan,
Nigeria.
Call: (+234) 8100938994
pulsepublishinghouse@ harvestways.org

PULSE Publishing House also avails you a secure processing and prompt worldwide shipment of orders primarily via www.harvestways.org

Other leading outlets include WHSmith.co.uk, Barnesandnoble.com & Amazon.com

www.ingramcontent.com/pod-product-compliance
Lightning Source LLC
Chambersburg PA
CBHW022216050726
47590CB00002B/822